THE BIG BOOK OF PLANT-BASED BABY FOOD

Adams Media
An Imprint of Simon & Schuster, Inc.
100 Technology Center Drive
Stoughton, MA 02072

First Adams Media trade paperback edition March 2021

ADAMS MEDIA and colophon are trademarks of Simon & Schuster.

For information about special discounts for bulk purchases, please contact Simon & Schuster Special Sales at 1-866-506-1949 or business@simonandschuster.com.

The Simon & Schuster Speakers Bureau can bring authors to your live event. For more information or to book an event contact the Simon & Schuster Speakers Bureau at 1-866-248-3049 or visit our website at www.simonspeakers.com.

Interior design by Sylvia McArdle
Interior photographs by Harper Point Photography

Manufactured in the United States of America

2 2022

Library of Congress Cataloging-in-Publication Data has been applied for.

ISBN 978-1-5072-1449-7
ISBN 978-1-5072-1450-3 (ebook)

THE BIG BOOK OF PLANT-BASED BABY FOOD

300 Healthy, Plant-Based Recipes Perfect for Your Baby and Toddler

TAMIKA L. GARDNER
Author of *201 Organic Baby Purées*

Adams Media

New York London Toronto Sydney New Delhi

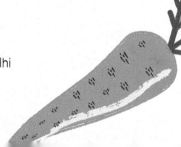

CONTENTS

PART 1: PLANNING FOR SUCCESS . . . 13

1

PLANT-BASED FOOD FOR BABIES:
THE BENEFITS OF EATING PLANTS . . . 14

2

YOUR PLANT-BASED KITCHEN . . . 23

3

BABY PURÉE ESSENTIALS: TIPS, TRICKS, AND
TECHNIQUES FOR HEALTHY HOMEMADE MEALS . . . 30

FIRST-STAGE MEALS:
SMOOTH PURÉES FOR BEGINNERS . . . 40

(6–7 MONTHS)

5

MORE FLAVOR TO SAVOR:
INTRODUCING SEMI-SMOOTH PURÉES . . . 90

(8–9 MONTHS)

PLEASING AN EXPANDED PALATE:
CHUNKY PURÉES FOR LITTLE ONES . . . 140
(10–12 MONTHS)

(continued on next page)

FUN AND FINGERLICIOUS FOOD:
TRANSITIONAL MEALS FOR TODDLERS . . . 190

(12+ MONTHS)

Apple Purée

Cherry Hand Pies

Fruity Yogurt Parfait

Avocado Smoothie Bowl

INTRODUCTION

WELCOME TO THE PLANT-BASED REVOLUTION!

As a parent, you have a huge responsibility in raising a human being, and that is no easy feat. The healthy food choices you make for your little ones today will help them make good food choices and live long, healthy lives free of sickness and disease. Strong immune systems, well-balanced diets, and long lives all start with you and the food choices you make for them.

The Big Book of Plant-Based Baby Food will help you see the importance of feeding your family plant-based foods and shows you how to continue on the path of plant-based eating as your baby gets older. The three hundred recipes in this book are all 100 percent plant-based (and most are also naturally gluten-free!). There is no meat, poultry, fish, seafood, or dairy ingredients—however, you can easily substitute or add in small amounts of animal products as you see fit. Each recipe features ingredients easily found in health sections of most supermarkets and grocery stores.

From purées to finger foods, the recipes in this book grow with your child well into the toddler years. Inside you'll find dishes like:

HOMEMADE BROWN RICE CEREAL

PEAR PURÉE

BRIGHT ZUCCHINI AND BROWN RICE

BLUEBERRY CREAM PIE

CINNAMON, APPLE, AND SWEET POTATO SURPRISE

CHICKPEA, CARROT, AND CAULIFLOWER MASH

HERBED CREAMED CORN

BABY RATATOUILLE

BANANA QUESADILLAS WITH RASPBERRY SAUCE

BEST-EVER PANCAKES

BAKED PITA CHIPS

NUTS BE GONE TRAIL MIX

With the help of this book, your children can enjoy fresh, sustainable, and healthy whole foods. You'll have creative control of every ingredient and texture and the peace of mind to know that, without animal-based products and highly processed food, your babies are on their way to a healthier life.

PLANNING FOR SUCCESS

Making your own plant-based baby food comes with many benefits and cost savings, and you'll be happy to know that it doesn't come with headaches and stress. Hopefully, as other moms and dads see how joyful you are in making plant-based meals for your little one, they will jump on the bandwagon and adopt the lifestyle too! Part 1 of this book will explain the core principles of a plant-based diet, its nutrition, and how you'll prepare purées. You'll also get tips on how to stock your kitchen and the basic equipment you need to plan for a successful start.

PLANT-BASED FOOD FOR BABIES:
THE BENEFITS OF EATING PLANTS

From the moment a child is born, she relies on her parents to give her everything she needs to develop and grow into a healthy, thriving adult. Fortunately, you can do this by providing your baby with the optimal nutrition she needs through plant-based foods!

PLANTS PROMOTE THE BEST HEALTH

There's no doubt that plants and whole foods provide the best nutrition for your body. As you probably learned in grade school, "you are what you eat." The American Academy of Pediatrics (AAP) agrees that babies should eat healthy and nutritious foods starting at six months of age, while avoiding added sugar and highly processed foods. What exactly is meant by "healthy and nutritious"? Fresh fruit, vegetables, legumes, grains, and foods that aren't created or produced in a factory provide all the essential nutrients that babies need to grow and stay healthy. According to the AAP, when a child reaches 9 months of age, there is a significant drop in fruit and vegetable consumption as the not so nutritious finger foods, snacks, and juices are introduced. This is the critical turning point when you can change the course of your child's eating habits and set them on the right path to great health as they grow and mature. When your baby eats a diet made up of mostly plant-based food and sticks with it throughout his life, he can reap some of the following benefits:

- A healthy body weight and composition
- Sense of well-being—great sleep, mental clarity, and positive moods
- Health insurance savings—fewer unplanned trips to the doctor and fewer medications
- Prevention of chronic ailments and diseases such as heart disease, cancer, and diabetes

How Eating Plants Promotes Good Health

Research and scientific studies show that a diet consisting of fruits, vegetables, legumes, and grains reduces the risks of many Western diseases that cause poor quality of life or even death. Consuming meat alone does not provide all the nutrition your body needs to function properly, and it doesn't offer the protection that plants provide. Humans can survive without eating meat, but the same doesn't hold true about plants. With the exception of vitamin B_{12}, plants provide all the essential vitamins, minerals, carbohydrates, and proteins you need to live a long healthy life. Plants also have superior healing and disease-prevention qualities that meat doesn't provide. The nutrient-dense, low-calorie profile of plants promotes healthy weight and great health overall with the following key components:

Antioxidants

Antioxidants consist of vitamins A, C, and E; minerals such as iron, zinc, copper, selenium, and beta-carotene; and flavonoids. Flavonoids are the biggest class of antioxidants and consist of healthy nutrients and chemicals found in plants. When you consume a variety of fruits and vegetables, your body will build up an entire defense team that works against free radicals, the unstable atoms that damage cells and cause disease. That's why it is so important to provide your baby a variety of foods to ensure he is getting an abundance of antioxidants.

Phytonutrients

Phytonutrients are compounds that are naturally found in plants such as fruits, vegetables, beans, grains, nuts, and seeds; they are potentially helpful in preventing chronic diseases. Phytonutrients may help strengthen the immune system, reduce inflammation, regulate hormones, and help repair and prevent damaged cells from reproducing. There are many types of phytonutrients that all have different roles in keeping your body healthy. Here are a few:

- **Flavonoids:** These inhibit tumor growth, reduce inflammation, and boost immunity. Flavonoids can be found in foods such as oranges, lemons, limes, apples, onions, and soybeans.

- **Carotenoids:** These inhibit cancer growth, support strong immunity, and promote healthy skin and vision. Beta-carotene, lycopene, lutein, and zeaxanthin are all types of carotenoids. Carrots, cooked tomatoes, leafy greens, sweet potatoes, broccoli, winter squash, apricots, cantaloupe, oranges, and watermelons all contain carotenoids.
- **Inositols:** Inositols prevent cell damage. Oats, rice, wheat, nuts, soybeans, and rye are a few sources.
- **Polyphenols:** Potent fighters against cancer formation and inflammation, polyphenols can be found in grapes, berries, citrus fruits, apples, whole grains, and peanuts.
- **Isoflavones:** These phytonutrients inhibit the growth of tumors and limit the production of cancer-related hormones. Typical sources are soybeans and soy products.

WHAT IS A PLANT-BASED LIFESTYLE?

A plant-based lifestyle is exactly what the name implies. There are no set rules or formal diet to follow, but it is a diet based on foods that naturally grow from the earth. Generally, people who consume plants and whole foods are satisfied and have their basic nutritional needs covered, and then some! Most of the calories, however, will come from starchy yet healthy foods such as potatoes, corn, peas; whole grains like brown rice and quinoa; and legumes such as chickpeas and beans to maintain satiety. These types of foods are misperceived to be bad for you because of their carbohydrate content. With this lifestyle, your baby will eat a variety of plant-based foods (although single ingredients in the beginning). The principles of a plant-based diet are:

- Focuses on eating plants and whole foods such as fruits, vegetables, legumes, seeds, nuts, and whole grains as the main source of nutrition
- Excludes refined and overly processed foods such as added sugar, processed oils, and white flour
- Limits or avoids animal consumption

TYPES OF PLANT-BASED DIETS

Vegetarianism and veganism are popular types of plant-based diets and support a plant-based lifestyle. However, a plant-based lifestyle is broader than these and offers more flexibility. People who follow a plant-based lifestyle may not consider themselves to be vegetarians or vegans. Here are a few examples of popular plant-based diets.

Vegetarianism

There are many facets to a vegetarian diet. The one thing that all vegetarians have in common is that they consume anything edible that grows from the earth. Fruits, vegetables, legumes, nuts, and herbs are common staples. Many vegetarians also include eggs and dairy in this type of diet, but meat is not allowed.

There are a few other variations of vegetarianism:

- **Ovo Vegetarianism:** This diet includes eggs and foods that contain eggs such as mayonnaise. It excludes all other animal-based products that contain anything derived from fish, poultry, seafood, and meat. Eggs provide macronutrients such as vitamin A and D. *Ovo* means "egg" in Latin.
- **Lacto Vegetarianism:** Following this plan includes consuming dairy products such as cow's milk, yogurt, and cheese. Eggs, meat, poultry, and seafood are excluded. Eating and planning meals that include iron, zinc, vitamin B_{12}, and omega-3 fatty acids are important with this type of diet to ensure a healthy supply of those nutrients. This lifestyle may help reduce cancer risk in adulthood, maintain a healthy weight, and promote a healthy heart over time. *Lacto* means "milk."
- **Lacto-Ovo Vegetarianism:** includes animal products like dairy and eggs. This type of vegetarian enjoys foods such as cheese, butter, and yogurt in addition to eggs. Fish, seafood, poultry, and meat are off limits. Like Lacto Vegetarians, it's important to include a balanced meal that includes foods that offer iron, zinc, vitamin B_{12}, and omega-3 fatty acids.

Veganism

Vegans avoid consuming and using animal products altogether. They do not consume animals, animal by-products, or honey, and they also believe in a cruelty-free lifestyle, meaning they do not wear fur, leather, wool, or down, and they also only wear cosmetics or other products that have not been tested on animals. This is the strictest form of a plant-based diet, but there are many benefits and rewards to choosing this type of lifestyle.

Mediterranean Diet

Inspired by traditional foods from Mediterranean countries, like Italy and Greece, this diet focuses on a high consumption of vegetables, fruits, healthy fats, nuts, beans, and whole grains. It also includes small amounts of red meat, dairy, and seafood.

Supplementing with Animal Products

If you decide to supplement your baby's diet with animal products, make sure to keep them to a minimum. Animal products should make up 10–20 percent of a total meal as a basic guideline. Remember to choose from local sources if you can and keep these parameters in mind:

- **Eggs:** choose free-range, organic if possible
- **Poultry:** choose free-range, organic if possible
- **Meat:** choose pastured or grass-fed
- **Seafood:** choose wild-caught from sustainable fisheries
- **Dairy:** choose organic from free-range, pasture-raised animals

A PLANT-BASED LIFESTYLE IS GOOD FOR THE PLANET

The effects of climate change are evident all around us on a daily basis, and the scientific evidence of their dangers is overwhelming. With this in mind, people around the world are making mindful choices to reduce their environmental impact. Switching to a plant-based diet will lower your carbon footprint and help you eat sustainably.

A review conducted by the Rockefeller Foundation-*Lancet* Commission on Planetary Health revealed that there is huge potential for humans to change their diets and consume more plants in order to improve health and reduce the environmental impacts of food production. The review also contained sixty-three studies that showed tremendous benefits to switching from a traditional Western diet to one containing more plants, including a 50 percent reduction in greenhouse gas emissions and land use. It is evident that a plant-based lifestyle can contribute to a healthier planet and curb the effects of climate change.

CHOOSE ORGANIC

Choosing organic foods offers another layer of health benefits for infants. According to the United States Environmental Protection Agency, babies who eat a diet consisting of plants that have little to no pesticide exposure are at less risk of developing neurological disorders, certain diseases, and other adverse health effects resulting from chemical exposure.

Organic foods are free from harmful pesticides, sewage sludge, hormones, genetic modification, artificial fertilizers, and antibiotics.

The United States Department of Agriculture (USDA) oversees the National Organic Program. Organic growers are inspected annually to ensure compliance with regulations that their products are produced using renewable resources and methods that sustain soil and water to protect the environment.

The Organic Labeling Program

The USDA helps consumers determine the authenticity of organic food and backs up these claims by labeling products with the USDA organic seal. When you see the round green and white label that says USDA ORGANIC, you'll know the product is free from pesticides, antibiotics, bioengineering, and hormones. To learn more about organic certification, visit www.usda.gov/topics/organic.

THE CLEAN FIFTEEN

Knowing what the cleanest plants are can help you shop smarter and reduce the amount of pesticides your baby will consume. The Environmental Working Group (EWG) is an advocacy group that annually ranks produce based on its pesticide load—meaning the amount of pesticides in food. Data used from the Food and Drug Administration and the United States Department of Agriculture help the EWG create these guidelines to help keep the public informed. The EWG's downloadable list ranks both the cleanest and the most pesticide-laden foods on their website at www.ewg.org/foodnews. The foods that rank at the top of the Clean Fifteen list are the safest to purchase from conventional farmers, as they have the least amount of pesticides.

THE DIRTY DOZEN

Based on research from the EWG, the fruits and vegetables at the top of the following Dirty Dozen list carry the heaviest load of pesticides when produced conventionally; therefore, try to purchase these items from organic suppliers. (To help you remember, these fruits and vegetables are bolded in the ingredient lists in the recipes in Part 2 of this book.)

THE CLEAN FIFTEEN

1. Avocados
2. Sweet corn
3. Pineapple
4. Onions
5. Papaya
6. Sweet peas (frozen)
7. Eggplant
8. Asparagus
9. Cauliflower
10. Cantaloupe
11. Broccoli
12. Mushrooms
13. Cabbage
14. Honeydew melon
15. Kiwi

THE DIRTY DOZEN

1. Strawberries
2. Spinach
3. Kale
4. Nectarines
5. Apples
6. Grapes
7. Peaches
8. Cherries
9. Pears
10. Tomatoes
11. Celery
12. Potatoes

Always thoroughly wash fruit and vegetables before eating them, including lemons and oranges, especially if you plan on using the skins for zest. Soaking and rinsing fresh produce in a bath of one part water, one part vinegar works the best to remove the dirt and pesticides.

GETTING ENOUGH ESSENTIAL VITAMINS AND NUTRIENTS

Although a plant-based lifestyle has many nutritional benefits and rewards, it's important to make sure your baby is getting enough of the essential nutrients like iron, calcium, vitamin B_{12}, and zinc. These nutrients are readily found in meat, but when conforming to a plant-based diet that minimizes or eliminates meat, it's important to consume plenty of foods that are rich in these key nutrients to make sure your baby is getting enough. A whole-foods, plant-based diet provides most of the nutrients and energy your baby needs for growth and development; however, talk to your pediatrician or pediatric dietician for advice regarding specific supplements your baby might need.

Vitamin B_{12}

Vitamin B_{12} is an important nutrient that can't be sufficiently obtained from a plant-based diet that excludes meat (unless including fortified foods). Vitamin B_{12} is only found in animal products including eggs, cheese, and milk, but even some animal products don't contain enough. Vitamin B_{12} comes from bacteria found in dirt. When animals eat dirt, they consume the bacteria that creates B_{12} and it's stored in the animals' tissues, which humans consume and benefit from. This also means that B_{12} is found in unwashed produce, but since most people wash their fruits and vegetables to prevent exposure to harmful parasites and pathogens, they wash away the vitamin too.

Vitamin B_{12} plays an important role in the body because it helps in the production of DNA and the development and protection of nerve cells. A deficiency in B_{12} can lead to many issues, including anemia, weakness, fatigue, difficulty concentrating, gastrointestinal issues, and more. This doesn't mean that you have to give your baby animal products. It just means that you may need to offer supplements and give foods such as cereals and plant-based products that are fortified with B_{12}.

Check a product's ingredient list to see if B_{12}, also known as cobalamin, has been added. Some fortified foods, like cereals, may even list the B_{12} amount on the Nutrition Facts panel. Just remember, Nutrition Facts show the percentage of the required daily amounts (RDA) of nutrients for adults. Infants will need less. (Infants 6 to 12 months need 0.5 micrograms per day of vitamin B_{12}, while adults need 2.4 micrograms.)

Vitamin D

Vitamin D is a chemical that your body makes when exposed to direct sunlight. It is needed for building healthy bones, and it helps keep your upper respiratory tract healthy. It is primarily found in fortified foods such as cereal and milk. The best way to make sure your baby is getting enough vitamin D is to expose his face, arms, and legs to the sun several times per week for as long as you are able, even if it's only a few minutes. If you aren't able to get outside, sitting in a sunny window may also help. Be careful not to pile on too much sunscreen, because although it's important, it decreases vitamin D production. If you live in an area where the UV index is under 3 any time of the year, you may want to consult your pediatrician to check your child's vitamin D levels during your wellness appointments. You can check the UV index by visiting www.epa.gov. Lack of vitamin D can cause mood disorders, severe asthma in children, cancer, and cardiovascular concerns. Unlike vitamin B_{12}, vitamin D is readily available by simply spending time outdoors in the sun.

Calcium

Calcium can only be absorbed in your bones when vitamin D is present. These two go hand in hand, so it's important to ensure your baby is getting enough vitamin D and calcium. Calcium is essential for building strong, healthy bones and teeth. Although we have been programmed to associate obtaining calcium from drinking cow's milk, humans don't need to drink cow's milk or consume any dairy products to get calcium. You can offer your baby (after she's reached 12 months of age) unsweetened calcium-fortified plant milk such as almond, oat, and coconut milk as part of a balanced diet.

Iron

Iron is an essential nutrient that's important for your baby's growth and development. Iron helps muscles store and move oxygen. Iron deficiency runs rampant in children, and the lack of it can cause impaired mental development. By the time babies are 6 months old, their iron stores are depleting rapidly, so it's important to offer plant-based foods that are rich in iron, including legumes, tofu, and green leafy vegetables.

Fats: Omega-3 Fatty Acids

Fat plays an integral part in your child's diet and should be incorporated into meals. Fat helps you feel satisfied after a meal and less likely to overeat. Breast milk and infant formula both contain lots of fat, and up until 12 months, it is a baby's primary fat source. According to the American Academy of Pediatrics, babies and toddlers under the age of two should obtain about 50 percent of their total caloric needs from fat and gradually reduce the amount at the age of two. Omega-3 and omega-6 essential fatty acids are vital for brain and visual development. Americans currently consume a lot more omega-6 fatty acids, which actually impairs the absorption of omega-3 fatty acids. It is important to have a balance. Omega-3s can be obtained from plants such as chia seeds, ground flaxseeds, kale, and tofu.

Zinc

Zinc is a trace mineral essential for normal growth and development and plays a role in keeping the immune system healthy. A deficiency in this important nutrient has been linked to increased colds and infections, learning disabilities, and impaired memory. Because of the low bioavailability of zinc in plants, people consuming a plant-based diet may need up to 50 percent more zinc than animal consumers. Zinc can be found in fortified cereals and plant-based yogurt, peas, lentils, sprouted beans, and tofu.

The following lists include foods high in these important vitamins and minerals.

VITAMIN C SOURCES
(TO BOOST ABSORPTION OF IRON):

- Bell peppers
- Broccoli
- Citrus (blended into foods starting at 10 months)*
- Kale
- Peas

IRON SOURCES:

- Almonds (crushed or blended into foods starting at 6 months)*
- Beans
- Dark leafy greens such as collard greens and kale
- Edamame
- Fortified grains and cereals such as oatmeal
- Lentils
- Pistachios (crushed or blended into foods starting at 6 months)*
- Tofu (starting at 8 months)

ZINC SOURCES:

- Cashews (blended into meals starting at 6 months)*
- Fortified organic cereals
- Lentils
- Peanut butter, smooth (starting at 6 months)*
- Peas
- Seeds

- Sprouted beans
- Tofu
- Whole grains

HOW TO OBTAIN VITAMIN D:

- Fortified plant-based milks and yogurts
- Time in the sun (20 minutes)

CALCIUM-RICH FOODS:

- Almond butter, smooth (starting at 6 months)*
- Beans, lentils, and chickpeas
- Edamame
- Fortified breakfast cereal
- Fortified plant milk (almond, coconut, oat, soy)
- Green leafy vegetables (broccoli, collard greens, kale)
- Sesame seeds
- Tahini
- Tofu

OMEGA-3 SOURCES:

- Chia seeds
- Flaxseeds

VITAMIN B$_{12}$ SOURCES:

- Fortified cereals
- Fortified nutritional yeast

The items on this list that are marked with an asterisk (*) are higher on the allergenic list and should only be introduced after less allergenic foods have been tolerated.

YOUR PLANT-BASED KITCHEN

It is time to stock the refrigerator, freezer, and pantry with all sorts of whole, plant-based foods that will make you feel great about making meals for your little one. The best part about a plant-based diet is that shopping is surprisingly simple and inexpensive. Your shopping cart will only consist of the healthiest foods around—fruits, vegetables, legumes, seeds, and whole grains.

Having a variety of foods available at all times will ensure your little eater gets all of his nutritional needs. You may find that your grocery trips are more frequent if you are opting for the freshest produce. Luckily, you can take advantage of online shopping and grocery pickup or delivery when you're short on time. It's also important to stock up on whole grains and complex carbohydrates for your little ones as they get older. The calories they need will come from the heavier, starchier foods such as potatoes, oats, and quinoa. Therefore, it's important to make sure you have plenty of complex carbs on deck. The more options you have on hand from fresh, frozen, and canned foods (such as pumpkin and beans), the easier it will be to prepare meals in a flash.

STOCKING FRESH FOODS

Fresh fruit and vegetables are the top choice if you plan to purée food for your baby within a day or two of purchase. However, keep in mind that imported produce is picked several days before it makes its way to the grocery store and likely sits in produce bins for several days before you arrive to shop. Therefore, subject everything you select to close scrutiny—make sure the melons are fragrant but firm, strawberries are plump and free from mold, and the beans look bright!

An abundance of fresh foods are available, especially when you visit your local farmers' market or specialty produce market. Some items will simply be unavailable frozen or in a can. You'll need to plan to spend time to shop and prepare those items. Additionally, you may decide to purchase all fresh fruit and vegetables, and if you do, kudos! It takes a lot of time to clean, prep, and cook fresh foods to purée, so be sure you are up for the task. You can also get great deals when you purchase in large bushels from the farmers' market. For example, you may be able to buy thirty pounds of sweet potatoes for $12 (which comes out to be .40 cents per pound) and can be shared with family or neighbors at that great price. Consider buying and processing fresh foods in bulk to make the most use of your time.

Buying from Famers' Markets and CSAs

If available in your area, an excellent option for purchasing fresh produce is at your local farmers' market or farm stand. This food contains more nutrients because it doesn't travel far (once produce is harvested, it loses vitamins and nutrients over time). Some farms even let you pick your own, which means you can take home a harvest straight from the source. It's a great experience for the entire family, and nothing's fresher than picking a bushel of apples off the tree yourself, like back in the old days. To find a list of farms in your area that offer this, visit www.pickyourown.org.

Another option for procuring fresh organic produce is through community-supported agriculture (CSA), which many farms offer. In a CSA, the consumer helps support the costs of growing the fruits and vegetables by purchasing a "share" or membership in the CSA. The cost is spread over payments made by the week, month, or growing season in exchange for a weekly box of fresh products straight from the farm. The box may include a variety of fruits, vegetables, or other farm products such as eggs and bread. Some CSAs even allow you to mix and match and make your own choices according to your preferences.

The CSA model helps many small farmers continue to farm, and revenue earned from the membership or share fees goes toward buying seed and the initial costs of planting, so the farmer does not have to wait for the harvest to collect money. This model allows the consumer to become directly involved in the food-production process. Another modern approach to a CSA is a produce delivery service such as www.theproducebox.com. Many people may not realize that a produce delivery service is a type of CSA and is extremely convenient because you place your order online, and deliveries come straight to your door. Check your local area to see if there is a delivery service available. To learn more about community-supported agriculture and how you can become involved, visit www.localharvest.org.

Growing Your Own

Another option is to make purées using fresh produce found right outside your door! Your own backyard or patio provides space and opportunity to grow organic produce. A small garden plot or a few containers are sufficient for a continuous harvest of herbs and other vegetables. This can be an inexpensive option to ensure that the organic tomatoes you love are just a few steps away. Designating a small garden plot in your backyard can create an abundance of salad greens, root vegetables, and herbs. It's important to purchase organic seeds, soil, fertilizer, and pest control (or make your own). You can even purchase elevated garden beds that are waist high, or self-watering container gardens that have ample space for herbs and vegetables and can be placed anywhere. There is no soil to dig up or remedy. Just start with a container and fresh dirt and you're good to go! Check out *Pinterest* and other online sites for DIY backyard gardening ideas.

BENEFITS OF FROZEN FOODS

If you want the benefits of fresh foods without the time expense, purchase frozen fruits and vegetables. Most of the first foods your baby will eat can be purchased frozen. Frozen foods are a great choice for making purées without worrying about your produce quickly going bad. It's easy to stockpile your freezer with a variety of fruit and vegetables, especially varieties that are out of season. That way your baby can enjoy the tastes of all seasons, and you can save yourself from making extra trips to the store.

Frozen foods are harvested and flash-frozen within 6 hours; therefore, many of the nutrients are well retained, and they may even have more of certain vitamins than fresh foods near the end of their life. All you have to do is steam or sauté the frozen foods and toss them in the food processor to purée. A few national organic brands include 365 Everyday Value (sold at Whole Foods), Woodstock, Stonyfield Organic, and Cascadian Farm Organic. If your schedule and life are busy, load up your freezer with a variety of frozen foods so that you have plenty to choose from when it's time to make a delicious meal.

CANNED FOODS

It's always a great idea to have canned foods on hand for convenience and in the event of an emergency. However, there is evidence that shows canned foods and some packaged foods are exposed to bisphenol A (BPA), a toxic, unregulated chemical used to line metal food and drink cans (including infant formula cans) and type #7 polycarbonate (PC) plastics. BPA is harmful to humans, even in low doses, and can cause serious health problems and diseases. Make sure the cans you purchase are BPA-free. If you are uncertain, contact the company directly to be sure. For more information on BPA, visit the Environmental Working Group's website at www.ewg.org/research/bisphenol.

Because purées are frozen or refrigerated, they are susceptible to spoiling when the refrigerator breaks down or if there is a power outage. For this reason, always keep an emergency stash of canned goods such as pears, green beans, corn, carrots, yams, and infant formula in your pantry. Canned beans, fruits, and vegetables are a good source of nutrition and can easily be prepared for the family and fork-puréed for baby in the event of an emergency. You might also consider having a day's worth of prepackaged organic, plant-based baby food in your diaper bag, just in case you get stuck with a flat tire or the visit to your mother-in-law's turns into a sleepover!

These days, busy moms and dads don't have time to slave over the stove stewing tomatoes or preparing beans. Fortunately, these items are best purchased in cans. Canned beans are an excellent source of protein, iron, and fiber, and they are easy to prepare—just open up the can and cook them! Tomato sauces and tomatoes are the number one choice for canned foods because they provide lycopene, an antioxidant that aids in cancer prevention. Research shows that lycopene is easily absorbed into the body because of the heat from the canning process. Therefore, purchase canned organic tomatoes and sauces to incorporate into baby purées. Make sure they are 100 percent plain tomatoes of any variety (diced, stewed, sauces, and so on) with no added sugar, salt, spices, or other ingredients.

Pumpkin is another canned staple. Having to cook pumpkins can take up precious time that you may not have. Therefore, pure canned pumpkin is great for incorporating in purées, muffins, yogurt, or pudding. Take care to buy pure pumpkin and not pumpkin pie filling, as the latter contains lots of sugar and is primarily used for baking pies.

While out on your shopping adventure, scour the aisles to see what is offered in the canned foods area. However, remember that canned foods, whether for babies or not, have been produced to last for years. Commercially canned food is heated to extreme temperatures and then cooled, which destroys many of the nutrients, and the taste doesn't come close to fresh. Purchase canned or jarred food, with the exception of tomatoes, beans, and pumpkin, as a last resort or to add to your emergency food supply.

KITCHEN COMMODITIES

Take stock of what fruit and vegetables you have in your refrigerator, freezer, and pantry, and then make a shopping list of other items that are included in the following lists. When your baby is young, you will only need single ingredients in fresh or frozen foods. Later on, you can add other foods to the list, including spices and healthy fats. Serve seasonal foods in all colors along with an array of whole grains and plant proteins to ensure your baby receives a well-balanced diet. Here are some suggestions for foods to keep on hand to make purées, finger food, and foods to keep on hand for an emergency situation. Stocking your pantry with these plant-based staples will allow you to whip up a variety of meals in a pinch!

FRESH PRODUCE (PICK IN-SEASON FROM THE LIST)

- Apples
- Apricots
- Avocados
- Bananas
- Beets (fresh or prepared)
- Broccoli
- Butternut squash and winter squash
- Carrots and parsnips
- Cauliflower
- Dates
- Lemons
- Limes
- Mangoes
- Nectarines
- Peaches
- Pears
- Plant-based milk (after age 8 months)
- Plums
- Potatoes (all varieties)
- Tofu
- Zucchini

FROZEN FOODS

- Bell peppers (red, green, or orange)
- Broccoli florets
- Cauliflower (florets or riced)
- Cherries
- Edamame
- Fruit blends
- Green beans
- Mangoes
- Peaches
- Spinach
- Sweet corn
- Sweet peas
- Vegetable medleys

CANNED FOODS

- Beans (black, pinto, kidney, baby lima, cannellini)
- Corn
- Green beans
- Pure pumpkin
- Tomatoes and tomato sauces
- Yams

SEASONINGS

- Dill
- Garlic powder
- Ground black pepper
- Ground cinnamon

- Ground ginger
- Ground nutmeg
- Onion powder
- Paprika (sweet or smoked)

- Salt (sea and/or kosher)
- Thyme
- Vanilla extract or paste (pure)

HERBS

- Basil
- Chives
- Dill

- Mint
- Oregano
- Parsley

- Rosemary

STOCKS (LOW-SODIUM VARIETIES OR HOMEMADE)

- Vegetable stock

OILS

- Avocado oil
- Extra-virgin coconut oil
- Extra-virgin olive oil

PANTRY PRODUCTS

- All-purpose unbleached flour
- Almond flour
- Applesauce (unsweetened organic)
- Beans and legumes (black beans, pinto beans, lentils, and split peas)
- Cereals (oatmeal, grits, granola, and muesli)
- Cornmeal
- Grains and seeds (barley, chia seeds, flaxseeds, quinoa, whole wheat couscous)

- Nut butters (sunflower seed, almond, and peanut—smooth varieties, only after other solid foods have been safely introduced between 6–8 months of age)
- Pasta (chickpea, black bean, edamame, or wheat)
- Rice (arborio rice, wild rice, and brown long-grain)

SAVE ON YOUR PLANT-BASED GROCERY BILL

In general, you can save money on a plant-based diet. The cost of beef, seafood, fish, and poultry is triple or quadruple the price per pound of fresh fruit, vegetables, and whole foods. Also, making homemade baby purées and meals is more cost-efficient than purchasing tiny jars and packages of commercial baby food.

Other ways to trim your family's overall grocery budget to ensure a continuous supply of plant-based foods include:

- **Clip/download coupons:** Collect newspapers and circulars and use coupons to save money on groceries and other household items you normally buy, such as toothpaste and laundry detergent. Or if your local stores support it, download their digital coupons for even easier savings. It's amazing how much you can save with a little planning.
- **Skip the prepared meals:** Nowadays supermarkets have sections that contain fully prepared meals or cook-your-own-food boxes. While most of those prepared meals contain some form of animal products, plant-based options are also available. These meals are offered at a premium price because most or all the work has been done for you. If you are looking to save on your grocery bill, skip these prepared options, hit the recipe sites, and make your own at home.
- **Grow your own:** Planting a garden is an inexpensive way to provide fresh organic produce for your dinner table. Many vegetables and berries can be grown with little effort in your backyard or even in containers on a small balcony or patio.
- **Buy in bulk:** A clever way to get the most for your money is to purchase fresh produce in bulk—the more you buy, the more you save. If you don't want or need a lot, share the cost with a friend or neighbor and split the harvest. Many warehouse stores, which require membership, offer fresh organic produce at cheaper prices than smaller stores.
- **Get the most out of the season:** Fresh produce that is in season is usually less expensive than foods that are not in season. Stock up on these goodies and purée and freeze the extra to extend the season and save money.

BABY PURÉE ESSENTIALS:
TIPS, TRICKS, AND TECHNIQUES
FOR HEALTHY HOMEMADE MEALS

When your baby has reached 6 months of age, you can safely introduce solid foods as long as she is showing signs she is ready and you have discussed starting solids with your pediatrician. Cooking meals for your baby is easy, fun, and rewarding. In this chapter you'll find the tools you need to get started, the requisites of food safety, and how to prepare and store baby purées. You'll learn all about making large quantities to freeze for later use and how to make the consistency perfect for your baby at each developmental stage.

EQUIPPED, ARMED, AND PREPARED!

If you go into any kitchen supply store, you will find a gadget for everything, which can add up really quickly if you try to buy it all! You probably already own all the things you need to make food for your baby. In addition, too many gadgets can overwhelm your kitchen with clutter, which will only drive you out of it. Keep your kitchen as serene as possible. Keep clutter off the counters and leave only the most commonly used practical items at hand. The first step to making food for your little one is making sure you are relaxed and ready for this great experience!

TOOLS OF THE TRADE

Here are some of the pieces of equipment that will become indispensable when making baby food:

- **Steamer basket:** A steamer basket fits nice and snug in a medium to large pot for steaming small batches of food. Many pots and pan sets come with a steamer basket. You can also use a rice or vegetable steamer if you have one on hand.
- **Fine-mesh stainless-steel strainer:** The holes in your pasta colander are too large to catch fine seeds and excess fibers that didn't get puréed enough for your infant to tolerate, but a strainer will do the trick. A stainless-steel strainer will resist rust and can last for years.
- **Food processor:** Although a blender could also be used, a food processor is truly the way to go, especially with a plant-based diet. Not only is it good for puréeing, the additional discs that come with it are great for slicing, julienning, and chopping fruit, vegetables, legumes, and nuts faster than you can blink an eye. It also kneads dough, which is handy if you're looking to make your own bread and baked goods. It's worth the investment and will likely get used more than any other kitchen gadget for food prep.
- **Immersion blender:** A immersion blender makes it easy to purée small meals in their own containers. Some also come with attachable containers that allow them to serve the same function as a mini food processor as well!
- **Spiralizer:** A spiralizer makes vegetable pasta out of foods such as zucchini, carrots, and potatoes. You'll need one of these if you want to make plant-based pasta such as zoodles. Most spiralizers come with different blades to make ribbons, spaghetti, and fettuccini "noodles."
- **Freezer-safe containers or ice cube trays:** You'll need something to store your purées in once they are made, and freezable glass containers (2–4 ounces) are the perfect solution. You can store single-ingredient purées in these and serve as is, or combine them to make other meals later on. Glass containers don't stain or hold smells, but other products on the market will work just as well. Choose whatever works best for you. Ice cube trays are handy for freezing purées in small portions that can be used later. Once frozen, pop them out and into storage bags for your freezer. Each ice cube–sized portion is equivalent to 2 tablespoons or about 1 ounce. The cubes can easily be mixed together, and you can grab as many as you need to make your desired portion. The best part about using ice cube trays is that they stack, they don't take up a lot of freezer space, and they are so inexpensive you can buy as many as you need for the amount of food you want to make. Be sure to label and date the storage bags so you know how long your purées have been in the freezer.

Nice-to-Have Tools

Here are some recommended (but not mandatory) tools for making baby purées:

- Large cutting board
- Santoku knife—great for chopping and slicing fruit and vegetables (if you don't have this type of knife, any knife will work!)

- Small paring knife—great for cutting and scoring fruits
- Vegetable peeler—to peel skins off vegetables (or use a knife to peel the old-fashioned way)
- Large slotted spoon—for transferring food
- Measuring cups and spoons—for measuring spices and ingredients
- Baking sheets—for baking vegetables (aluminum foil works perfectly if you don't have these)
- Stock pot—for making vegetable broth or cooking large amounts of food
- 2-quart saucepan—for smaller batches
- 12" nonstick skillet—for sautéing
- Baking dishes
- Large colander and mixing bowl—for rinsing and cleaning produce
- Permanent marker and labels for labeling

As you can see, making and preparing healthy food for your baby doesn't require a large investment. You may find that you only need a few items from the previous list. How wonderful is that?

Other Supplies

In addition to the previously mentioned items, you'll need feeding supplies for your little one. Keep a few bibs, small bowls, and baby spoons handy to start off. As your baby starts to self-feed, you can upgrade to plates with dividers and forks. Many stores offer melamine bowls and plates for children. Melamine is not microwave-safe, so take care to always heat your baby's food

in a glass dish and transfer the food to your child's plate.

If your budget allows, invest in a high chair that your baby can use until well after his first year. The best high chairs are ones that can be strapped around a standard dining-room chair so that it doesn't take up additional space. Some high chairs make it difficult for a baby to sit at the table in small living quarters, and it's important that your baby share meals with you and the rest of the family. This will help establish a healthy eating routine at an early age.

SAFETY FIRST

It's important to practice safe hygiene every time you make a meal. Contaminated counters, appliances, and feeding supplies are a sure way to drive you insane—and possibly send everyone you've fed to the hospital. Safe food-handling practices are a must for preparing baby purées or any food that you make. Follow these tips to reduce the risk of contamination and illness.

- Always wash your hands for 20 seconds with warm, soapy water before and after handling food. Make sure you clean your wrists and under your nails.
- Frequently clean the areas where you prepare food—including counters, sinks, faucets, and floors—with an eco-friendly cleaning solution.
- Separate meat and poultry from other food items if your household occasionally uses meat products. In fact, keep two

separate and distinct cutting boards for meat and plant-based products.

- Wash cutting surfaces with hot, soapy water after each use. Cross-contamination can occur when you place cooked meat or produce on surfaces contaminated by raw meat.
- Always cook food to proper temperatures. Use a meat thermometer to make sure meat is completely done.
- Refrigerate your food right away so bacteria cannot grow on the food. Don't let the food sit out on the counter!

Following these safety guidelines will ensure the health and safety of your family.

COOKING TECHNIQUES

There are many ways to cook purées for your baby. Knowing the pros and cons of your appliances will help you decide which to use to cook foods thoroughly. When deciding on a cooking technique, consider the season and the reason. For example, if it's cold outside and you're swamped with things to do, consider baking. Or, if you planned on making steamed broccoli for the family, you might decide to steam apples or cauliflower for your baby while the pot is already out. The following are commonly used cooking methods for making baby purées.

Baking

Baking helps food retain the most nutrients but takes the longest to cook foods until tender, especially potatoes and squash.

However, while the food is in the oven, you can get other things accomplished around the house. Because of the oven's large capacity, you can bake up to four different dishes simultaneously, making it easy to prepare a couple of months' worth of food. For example, you can bake sweet potatoes, squash, apples, and eggplant at the same time. If you have a double oven, you can even double that amount!

Steaming

Steaming preserves more nutrients and antioxidants than boiling or microwaving. Therefore, it is a good way to cook fruits, vegetables, and a variety of other foods. To steam using a pot and steaming basket, simply fill the pot with about an inch of water (make sure the water does not touch the bottom of the basket). Bring the water to a boil over medium-high heat, add the food to the basket, and cover tightly. If you don't have a steaming basket, you can still "steam" by adding about 2 tablespoons of water to the pot, cover, and cook over medium-low heat. You'll find that most foods cook quickly using this method. Steam until the fruit or vegetable is pierced easily with a fork.

Microwaving

Microwaving is quick and convenient for cooking many fruits, vegetables, and cereals. With microwave cooking, there are definite space limitations—you can only cook small batches. In addition, microwaves can cause hot spots in foods resulting in uneven cooking and an unintentional food explosion if you aren't careful to allow the steam to escape by poking holes in foods with high water content or stirring purées or foods like oatmeal frequently. Therefore, use it as a last resort for cooking and reheating foods for your baby. If you are going to reheat food, reduce the power to 50 percent to reduce hot spots.

Consider these additional warnings when using the microwave. First, never heat up food in plastic dishes or in plastic wrap not marked "microwave-safe." Research has shown that the toxic chemicals in plastic can leach into the food during microwaving, causing long-term detrimental effects. Look on the bottom of a plastic dish to see if it is marked as microwave-safe. If you are unsure, play it safe and don't use the dish in the microwave. Instead, use a glass dish. Second, never heat up food covered in aluminum foil or leave metal eating utensils in the bowl. That is a quick way to send your kitchen up in flames!

Boiling

Boiling is the least beneficial cooking method, so turn to it as a last resort. Studies show that about 50 percent of foods' nutrients seep into the water during the cooking process. Many people don't know this and pour the remaining nutrient-rich liquid down the drain. Now that you're equipped with this important knowledge, be sure to incorporate the remaining liquid into your purées, should you decide to use this cooking method.

IT'S ALL ABOUT CONSISTENCY

There are three types of baby purée consistencies—smooth, semi-smooth, and chunky. The consistency you make your purées will depend on your baby's development.

Stage 1: Smooth Purées

A smooth purée is appropriate for babies just starting to eat solids, at around 6 months of age. Smooth purées are free of bumps, lumps, and fibrous materials. They are similar to the consistency of plain yogurt or commercial stage 1 baby food. Your food processor will achieve this smoothness with water or other liquids added. The purée will eventually resemble a whirlpool while being processed, which is a good indicator of a smooth texture. Starchy foods such as potatoes may require added water, while some foods that naturally retain water, like pears, may not need any additional liquid. Therefore, turn on the purée function first and then gradually add liquid in small quantities at a time to achieve a smooth texture.

Stage 2: Semi–Smooth Purées

The semi-smooth consistency is smooth like yogurt but with small chunks of food here and there to help babies around 8 months old learn to chew. These tiny chunks of soft food can be things like rice, pasta, and diced cooked vegetables. The semi-smooth consistency is comparable to commercial stage 2 baby food. A good way to achieve a semi-smooth consistency is to add minced pieces of cooked, soft foods to a smooth purée.

Stage 3: Chunky Purées

The final consistency is chunky. You can achieve a chunky consistency with the "pulse" feature on your food processor or blender, or you can also purée to a smooth consistency and then add diced chunks of fruit, vegetables, or pasta back in. A chunky consistency is comparable to commercial stage 3 baby food.

Purchasing these three stages of commercial baby food will give you some idea of what the purées are like at each stage. Don't be afraid to take a taste. After all, it will be a great reminder of why you are making baby food in the first place!

Tweaking Purées

With your first few attempts of making purées, it is possible to make simple mistakes like adding too much liquid or not adding enough. If this happens to you, don't start over. It is not necessary to throw out the food because it is not the right consistency. Instead, try making these few minor adjustments to get the consistency just right.

- **Thinning:** If your purée is too thick, try thinning it out by adding filtered water, vegetable stock, or by using any leftover liquid from steaming or boiling. You may also use fresh breast milk or formula for an added nutritional boost, although keep in mind it will alter the flavor of your purées. However, if you plan on freezing the purée, don't add formula or previously frozen breast milk. Most of the recipes in this book will call for water for thinning. Feel free to substitute whatever of the aforementioned liquids you see fit.

- **Thickening:** To thicken purées that are too thin, you can add more cooked food if you have more, or add cooked infant cereal such as quinoa or oatmeal. Quinoa takes on the flavor of whatever it's cooked with. However, there are other foods that can be used as thickeners such as mashed potatoes, plant-based yogurt, wheat germ, or ground flaxseeds. Make sure that whatever you add has already been introduced to your baby.

- **Sweetening:** Some purées may be too bitter for your baby's liking. There are ways you can sweeten your purées using whole foods instead of refined cane sugar. Try not to overdo it on sweetening; use just enough to offset any bitter taste, rather than making purées sweeter than they naturally are. To sweeten purées, you can add a ripe banana, strawberries, date purée, or 100 percent organic fruit juice. Make sure your baby has already been introduced to those foods prior to adding.

It is also important to check the purée to make sure there are no unprocessed chunks. Some foods are naturally lumpy or grainy, but as long as there are no actual chunks or fibrous material, it should be safe to proceed with feeding.

BIG-BATCH PURÉE PREP STEP-BY-STEP

With a little planning, your time shopping and in the kitchen can pay off, and you'll be whipping up batches of nutritious plant-based purées with ease! Follow these five simple steps for making big batches of single-ingredient purées.

Step 1: Schedule Time

The best thought-out plan will result in a hassle- and stress-free chef! Therefore, set the time aside for grocery shopping and making purées for your baby each week, month, or whatever interval you choose. Don't schedule these tasks on days when you have other things to do or are pressed for time. Schedule a grocery day and a purée day separately. Shopping for the best foods will be more time-consuming than you think, because you will want to find the ripest pear or the freshest bananas. By the time you get home from shopping you may be too exhausted to prep and purée too. But if you've got the energy and ambition, there is no point in putting off for tomorrow what you can do today!

Step 2: Go Shopping

Shopping for plant-based food can be a great outing for everyone to enjoy. But how much should you buy? To make a big batch that will last a month or two, start out with about two pounds of foods that can be cooked and frozen, such as sweet potatoes, green beans, squash, and so on. For perishable foods, such as bananas and avocado, purchase a couple initially, and plan to serve those foods fresh. Plan to replenish the perishable foods as soon as they are consumed. Once you get going, you'll be able to gauge how much your baby eats and can plan your future shopping trips accordingly.

Step 3: Food Preparation

Turn up the music or tune in to your favorite show for this step. There will be a lot to do if you've purchased fresh produce. If you can, get your other family members involved in the prep work to help move things along.

Here is how you will prepare most fresh fruits and vegetables for puréeing:

1. Wash each food thoroughly. Use a large bowl with one part water and one part distilled white vinegar for soaking. Rinse everything well and pat to dry with paper towels or a clean kitchen towel.

2. Remove all peels, seeds, and cores. Leave potatoes and squash unpeeled for baking or roasting.

3. Trim ends and remove all inedible parts (such as stems, cores, and seeds).

4. For fruits and vegetables that require steaming, cut into halves or quarters.

Step 4: Cook

Cook everything using your preferred cooking method, taking into account the tips in the Cooking Techniques section earlier in this chapter.

Step 5: Purée and Freeze

Purée foods one ingredient at a time in a blender or food processor. Make sure to thoroughly rinse the food processor or blender between purées. Spoon purées into freezing jars or ice cube trays if using, leaving just a little room near the top for the purée to expand once frozen. Cover with the lids or use plastic wrap and freeze. If using ice cube trays, remove the purée cubes after 24 hours and transfer to freezer-safe bags. Label and freeze for 8 to 12 weeks.

FREEZING AND THAWING HOMEMADE PURÉES

Freezing your baby purées ensures that you'll have plenty of food for the coming months. A little time spent up front will give you a freezer well stocked with a variety of fruits and vegetables for up to 12 weeks! You won't spend hours in the kitchen each day or even each week. Just a few hours a month is all you need to prepare a couple of months' worth of baby food.

To get started, you'll need several ice cube trays, plastic wrap, freezer bags, and a permanent marker or label. When your purées have been cooked and cooled, spoon the mixture into the ice cube trays and repeat this process for each type of food. However, freeze only one type of food per tray. Otherwise, you may forget what you've added.

Recommendations for freezing times to maintain freshness:

- Fruit and vegetable purées—up to 3 months
- Grains (such as rice and quinoa)—up to 6 months
- Legumes and beans—up to 6 months
- Pasta and breads—up to 6 months

Thawing

Use any of the following methods for safely thawing frozen baby purées. Consume the food within two days after thawing. Do not refreeze.

- **Refrigerator method:** Thaw your baby purées overnight. If you are using purée cubes place them in a separate covered bowl until serving.
- **Water bath method:** For faster thawing, make a water bath! Simply place the covered container or storage bag in a larger bowl of warm water until the food is thawed.
- **Microwave method:** Place the frozen cubes in a microwave-safe bowl and use the defrost setting on your microwave to thaw, or reduce the power to 30 percent. If your purées were already frozen in a microwave-safe container, simply pop it in and use the previously mentioned settings.

PART 2

PLANT-BASED PURÉES FOR EACH AGE

Every baby develops at his own pace in his own unique way. Your child will undergo rapid growth and development each month. Now is the time to take out your camera to capture these precious moments! In the following chapters you'll find recipes for the four feeding stages. Your child will acquire new skills in each stage to prepare him for the next. Food purées will go from smooth and runny to diced foods your child can pick up and feed himself. Pay attention to your child's developmental stages and feed according to the skills he has.

4

FIRST-STAGE MEALS:
SMOOTH PURÉES FOR BEGINNERS
(6-7 MONTHS)

At this point in your baby's development, there's a whole new world outside of breast milk or formula for him to explore. From the age of 6 months, your baby is able to experience his first taste of solid food. This chapter introduces basic purées consisting of single ingredients for your baby to discover. At this stage, start off with smooth purées that run off the spoon and then gradually thicken to a yogurt-like consistency. Introduce foods one at a time (in any order), and wait a day or two before introducing another one. If your baby displays any signs of an allergic reaction, such as rash, swelling, difficulty breathing, vomiting, or diarrhea, discontinue all foods in question and contact your family physician immediately for further instruction. Once your child has tolerated a food, try offering a new single-ingredient food and repeat the process. You can then combine foods that have been tolerated for additional flavor and texture.

Single-ingredient purées and iron-fortified infant cereals such as oatmeal and barley are a great introduction to the new world of food. Babies need foods rich in iron and fat for healthy brain development. Alternatively, avocados, potatoes, plant-based yogurt, bananas, pears, and apples are popular among babies because of these foods' mild, sweet taste.

If your baby doesn't seem interested in a particular food, continue to offer the food a few days later and keep repeating this process until she accepts the new taste. He may initially take a tablespoon or so before he is satisfied; however, his appetite and interest will increase over a short period of time.

HOMEMADE QUINOA CEREAL

Quinoa is naturally rich in iron and also has magnesium, folate, manganese, and zinc, among other nutrients. Because of its abundant nutrition profile, it is an excellent choice when introducing solids. You can purchase white, red, or black quinoa to make this nutritious cereal. Try experimenting with them all separately or mix them.

Yields 10 servings

1 cup plus 3 tablespoons water, divided
½ cup quinoa (any variety)

1. In a small saucepan over medium-high heat, add 1 cup water and bring to a boil. Add quinoa, stir, and reduce heat to low. Cover and cook 10–12 minutes until all the water is absorbed and quinoa is fluffy. Remove from heat and allow to cool about 5 minutes.

2. Transfer quinoa to a food processor and add 3 tablespoons water. Purée until smooth and slightly runny. If the mixture is still thick and not quite running off the spoon, continue adding water a tablespoon at a time to achieve desired consistency. Serve immediately.

FIRST CEREALS

Quinoa, oatmeal, barley, and brown rice are all excellent grains that can be prepared into cereals and introduced to your baby as long as she is developmentally ready. Feel free to serve them in any order and blend them with other single-ingredient purées as your baby advances to other foods.

HOMEMADE BROWN RICE CEREAL

New guidance suggests that rice cereal should be given sparingly due to arsenic concerns. But because it is easily digested and has a low likelihood of causing an allergic reaction, it's a good choice as a first food. Serve it with other single-ingredient purées or mix it with the other cereals mentioned in this book (oatmeal, quinoa, barley) for a milder taste while getting the nutritional benefits of the other grains. To get more iron, add wheat germ prior to cooking.

Yields 3 servings

¼ cup brown rice
1 cup water
1 tablespoon wheat germ

1. Using either a food processor or coffee bean grinder, grind rice into a fine powder.

2. In a small saucepan over medium-high heat, add water and bring to a boil.

3. Add rice powder and wheat germ to boiling water. Stir constantly, about 30 seconds.

4. Reduce heat to low. Cover and simmer 7–8 minutes until mixture is a smooth, thick consistency. Stir occasionally to prevent sticking.

5. Let cool to lukewarm. Thin with additional water if needed to achieve desired consistency. Serve immediately.

IRON IN HOMEMADE CEREALS

Never add iron supplements to your cereals, as too much iron can be harmful to babies (as well as adults). Adding wheat germ is perfectly safe, or you can even mix your cereal with another grain that naturally has a lot of iron, such as quinoa or oats. You can even mix it with instant grits, which are fortified with iron.

HOMEMADE OATMEAL CEREAL

This type of cereal starts with grinding oats into a powder, which creates a runnier consistency for babies who aren't ready for a thicker texture. If your baby can handle a thicker texture, see Pear Oatmeal in Chapter 5.

Yields 3 servings

¼ cup old-fashioned oats (not quick-cooking)
1 cup water

1. Using either a food processor or coffee bean grinder, grind oats into a fine powder.

2. In a small saucepan over medium-high heat, add water and bring to a boil.

3. Add powdered oats, stirring constantly, about 30 seconds.

4. Reduce heat to low, cover, and simmer 8–10 minutes until oats are smooth and slightly runny. Stir occasionally to prevent sticking and burning.

5. Remove from heat and cool to lukewarm. Thin with additional water if needed to achieve desired consistency. Serve immediately.

HOMEMADE BARLEY CEREAL

Another great solid food introduction, barley boasts fiber, iron, manganese, and B vitamins, all essential for healthy development. Barley does contain gluten, so watch out if your family has a history of celiac disease and consult with your pediatrician before feeding.

Yields 3 servings

¼ cup uncooked barley
1½ cups water

1. Using either a food processor or coffee bean grinder, grind barley into a fine powder.

2. In a small saucepan over medium-high heat, add water and bring to a boil.

3. Add ground barley, stirring constantly, about 30 seconds. Reduce heat to low.

4. Cover and simmer 15–20 minutes until all the water is absorbed. Stir to prevent sticking.

5. Remove from heat and cool to lukewarm. Thin with additional water if needed. Serve immediately.

APPLE PURÉE

Honeycrisp, Pink Lady, and Gala apples make particularly good apple purée, though any variety can be used. Apples are among one of the few fruits that you can find year-round, and there is little concern with allergies. This fruit is a particular favorite among babies and provides protection against some cancers, helps keep teeth healthy, and helps keep digestion moving smoothly.

Yields 10–12 servings

4 medium apples, peeled, cored, and chopped (any variety)

2 tablespoons water

1. In a medium saucepan over low heat, combine apples and water.

2. Cover and cook about 10 minutes until tender.

3. Transfer apples with water to a food processor and purée until smooth. Thin with additional water if needed to achieve desired consistency. Serve warm or chilled.

DO THE APPLES HAVE TO BE COOKED?

Yes and no. Cooking apples ensures they're soft enough for babies to eat. While there are some schools of thought that babies can start weaning with very small pieces of diced food, every baby develops differently. If your baby shows signs at 6 months that he can handle bits of raw apple, it won't hurt him. Just make sure the variety of apple is softer in texture (not a crispy variety) and mash it really well with a fork. If you can't mash it with a fork, it may be too tough for your baby to gum. Stick to cooking it first if this is the case.

SWEET PEA PURÉE

Sweet peas burst with flavor and pair well with other vegetables such as carrots, cauliflower, and potatoes. If you can find fresh peas, use them. If you can't, purchase frozen peas, as some canned varieties may contain added salt or even sugar. Sweet peas are a great introduction to solid foods, as they contain protein, iron, fiber, and many vitamins.

Yields 4 servings

1 cup water
1 cup fresh or frozen sweet peas

1. In a medium saucepan over medium-high heat, add water and bring to a boil. Add peas to a steamer insert and set into saucepan. Cover and steam about 10 minutes until tender.

2. Using a slotted spoon, transfer steamed peas to a food processor (reserve the cooking liquid for thinning). Process until smooth. Add a little of the reserved water if needed to achieve desired consistency. Serve warm.

SWEET POTATO PURÉE

Sweet potatoes are loaded with antioxidants. Whether cooked on the stovetop or baked in the oven, sweet potatoes purée magnificently, and it is easy to make them the perfect consistency using a fork instead of a food processor. Keep plenty of these carotene-rich wonders on hand; they'll keep longer than fruit and other vegetables.

Yields 8–10 servings

2 large sweet potatoes

1. Preheat oven to 350°F. Pierce sweet potatoes in random spots with a fork.

2. Place sweet potatoes on a baking sheet and bake about 45 minutes until potatoes start to pucker and are easily pierced with a fork. Let cool 15 minutes.

3. Slice each potato in half and scoop out the flesh into a food processor.

4. Purée while gradually adding water, if needed, to achieve desired consistency. Serve warm.

BANANA PURÉE

Use bananas that have started spotting—this means they are ripe and easy to mash. Make this recipe as an on-demand purée to be consumed immediately. To make a big batch of banana purée to freeze for later, use a food processor to do all the work. Simply peel the bananas, drizzle a little lemon juice on them to keep them from turning brown, and process until smooth.

Yields 1 serving

½ **large ripe banana, peeled**

In a small bowl, add the banana. Using a fork, mash until smooth and creamy. Serve immediately.

AVOCADO PURÉE

Avocado is a great first food and provides amazing health benefits for baby. It's loaded with monounsaturated fat (the "good" fat), folate, iron, potassium, fiber, and more. Because of the fat and high-calorie content of avocado, your baby needs only about 2 tablespoons per serving. Ripened avocados don't require any kitchen equipment, just a fork!

Yields 1 serving

1 medium ripe avocado, halved
Few drops lime juice

1. Scoop out 2 or 3 tablespoons of flesh from one half of the avocado and add it to a small bowl.

2. Mash with a fork until smooth and creamy. Add a few drops of lime juice to prevent the mash from oxidizing and turning brown. Serve immediately.

3. Wrap remaining avocado with the pit in it with plastic wrap and refrigerate for later use. Leaving the pit in the fruit will prevent the avocado from oxidizing and keep it fresh longer.

KNOW WHEN IT'S RIPE

When you pick an avocado to serve to your baby, choose one that is soft when you press firmly on the skin in several places. This makes the best mashed purée. If the avocado is hard and doesn't give, it's not ripe enough for mashing.

CUCUMBER PURÉE

Cucumber has a mild yet interesting flavor that babies enjoy. Make big batches of this purée to freeze because it's meant to be mixed later on with cereals, plant-based yogurt, fruit, and other vegetable purées. English cucumbers are extra-long and their seeds are small and chewable, making prepping easy. If you choose a traditional cucumber, be sure to remove the seeds before puréeing.

Yields 4 servings

2 medium English cucumbers, peeled and chopped

Transfer cucumbers to a food processor. Process until smooth. To serve, combine with infant cereal or freeze for combining with other purées in the next stage.

PEACH PURÉE

Fresh peaches require a bit of prepping before puréeing. To save time, you can buy frozen sliced peaches. Remember you will pay a lot more for that convenience. Purchasing frozen fruit and vegetables is also a great way to get produce out of season.

Yields 4 servings

5 medium peaches
8 cups water

1. With a small paring knife, score a cross on the bottom of each peach. This will make peeling easier.

2. In a medium pot over medium-high heat, bring water to a boil. Submerge peaches in boiling water for 1 minute. If the water is not covering the peaches, add more until they are completely submerged. Remove from heat and, leaving peaches in the pan, allow to cool to room temperature.

3. Starting from the cut, peel the skin away from the fruit and pull the flesh away from the pit. Discard peels and pits.

4. Transfer peaches to a food processor. Process until smooth. Add water a little at a time to achieve desired consistency. Serve warm or chilled.

NECTARINE PURÉE

Check out your local farmers' market in the summer and stock up on nectarines for this sweet purée. Nectarines are rich in beta-carotene, vitamin C, potassium, and niacin. Nectarines and peaches are natural constipation relievers, due to their high fiber content.

Yields 15 servings

5 medium nectarines
8 cups water

1. With a small paring knife, score a cross on the bottom of each nectarine. This will make peeling easier.

2. In a medium saucepan over medium-high heat, bring water to a boil. Submerge nectarines in boiling water for 1 minute. If water is not covering the nectarines, add more until they are completely submerged. Remove from heat and, leaving nectarines in the pan, allow to cool to room temperature.

3. Starting from the cut, peel the skin away from the nectarine and pull the flesh away from the pit. Discard peels and pits.

4. Transfer nectarines to a food processor. Process until smooth. Add water a little at a time to achieve desired consistency. Serve warm or chilled.

PEACH? NECTARINE? WHAT'S THE DIFFERENCE?

Both of these are stone fruits, but the major difference is that a peach is larger and has a fuzzy outer skin, while nectarines are usually smaller, smooth on the outside, and sweeter. There is a slight difference in taste, but they can be used interchangeably in recipes.

PEAR PURÉE

Pears are very sweet and make a runny consistency when puréed. Therefore, you can also mash ripe pears with a fork to maintain some texture or to add back into the purée to thicken it. Make sure the pears are soft to touch to ensure they are fully ripened. To know for sure, try a piece for yourself to determine if it's suitable for mashing. Pears contain soluble fiber, which aids in digestion and can help relieve constipation.

Yields 6 servings

4 medium ripe pears, peeled, cored, and chopped

1 tablespoon water

1. In a medium saucepan over medium-low heat, add pears and water.

2. Cover and cook about 7 minutes until tender. Stir frequently.

3. Transfer pears to a food processor. Process until smooth. Serve warm or chilled.

PRUNE PURÉE
(PICTURED)

Prunes are an amazing source of fiber, providing 2 grams of fiber per ounce. Adding prunes to your baby's diet will help her maintain a healthy gastrointestinal tract and regular bowel movements. Baby constipated? Give her prunes!

Yields 15 servings

2 cups dried pitted prunes

1. In a large bowl, combine prunes and enough boiling water to cover. Cover with a lid or aluminum foil and soak the fruit 15–20 minutes until it's soft and plump.

2. Using a slotted spoon, transfer prunes to a food processor. Process until completely smooth and no fibrous material remains. Add water a little at a time if needed to achieve desired consistency. Serve warm or chilled.

PLUM PURÉE

Picking the perfect plum is the most important part of this recipe. Choose a plum that is already ripe; it should be soft when you press it. Picking plums that are not ripe enough will result in a bitter, coarse purée.

Yields 15 servings

8 cups water
5 medium plums

1. With a small paring knife, score a cross on the bottom of each plum. This will make peeling easier.

2. In a medium saucepan over medium-high heat, bring water to a boil. Submerge plums in boiling water for 1 minute. If water is not covering the plums, add more until they are completely submerged. Remove from heat and, leaving plums in the pan, allow to cool to room temperature.

3. Starting from the cut, peel the skin away from the plum and pull the flesh away from the pit. Discard peels and pits.

4. Transfer plums to a food processor. Process until smooth. Add water a little at a time to achieve desired consistency. Serve warm or chilled.

SPLIT PEA PURÉE

Split peas are a great source of protein, fiber, and iron. Combine this purée with mashed potatoes and add a dab of plant-based butter for a more savory meal. And if you are already prepping those peas, why not make split pea soup for lunch?

Yields 4 servings

½ cup dried green split peas, picked and rinsed
1 cup water

1. In a small saucepan over medium-high heat, combine split peas and water. Bring to a boil.

2. Reduce heat, cover, and simmer 30–45 minutes until tender. Remove from heat.

3. Using a slotted spoon, transfer peas to a food processor (reserve the cooking liquid for thinning). Process until smooth. Add a little of the reserved water if needed to achieve desired consistency. Serve warm.

EGGPLANT PURÉE

Eggplant is an excellent source of fiber and contains cancer-preventing antioxidants. It comes in many varieties; you can choose any kind for this recipe. Freeze any leftovers to combine with other purées.

Yields 15 servings

1 medium eggplant, peeled and chopped

1. In a large pot over medium-high heat, combine eggplant and enough water to cover. Bring to a boil.

2. Reduce heat to low and simmer 10–12 minutes until tender. Remove from heat. Cool slightly.

3. Using a slotted spoon, transfer eggplant to a food processor (reserve the cooking liquid for thinning). Process until smooth. Add a little of the reserved water if needed to achieve desired consistency. Serve warm.

GREEN BEAN PURÉE

Unless you are building an emergency stash, stay away from canned green beans, since nutritional value is lost in the canning process. Stick to fresh or frozen green beans for the best nutrition. For a tastier purée, you can add cooked vegetable stock to the food processor when thinning instead of water.

Yields 8 servings

1 cup water
4 cups trimmed and cut green beans

1. In a medium saucepan over medium-high heat, add water and bring to a boil. Add beans to a steamer insert and set into saucepan. Cover and steam about 10 minutes until tender.

2. Using a slotted spoon, transfer beans to a food processor and reserve the liquid for thinning. Process until smooth. Add a little of the reserved water if needed to achieve desired consistency. Serve warm.

NOT SMOOTH ENOUGH?

If your food processor didn't do the job of puréeing until completely smooth, you can transfer the mixture to a fine-mesh strainer and push the purée through with the back of a spoon to separate the chunky bits from the purée.

ZUCCHINI PURÉE

Zucchini is one of those versatile vegetables that takes on the flavor of other foods because of its mild taste. It's a great first food loaded with beta-carotene, potassium, vitamin C, and folate. Zucchini can easily be grown in your backyard. One plant can provide enough zucchini to feed your baby for many months! It is not necessary to peel zucchini; however, you may do so if you choose.

Yields 2 servings

1 cup water
1 cup sliced zucchini

1. In a medium saucepan over medium-high heat, add water and bring to a boil. Add zucchini to a steamer insert and set into saucepan. Cover and steam about 10 minutes until tender.

2. Using a slotted spoon, transfer zucchini to a food processor (reserve the cooking liquid for thinning). Process until smooth. Add reserved water as needed to achieve a smooth consistency. Serve warm.

BROCCOLI PURÉE

Broccoli is a terrific food for babies because it is packed with vitamin C, potassium, and folate. Try serving broccoli and cauliflower together for an even tastier meal when your baby is ready for new tastes. This recipe uses frozen broccoli florets, which will save prep time; however, fresh can always be used!

Yields 6 servings

1 cup water
2 cups frozen broccoli florets

1. In a medium saucepan over medium-high heat, add water and bring to a boil. Add broccoli to a steamer insert and set into saucepan. Cover and steam about 10 minutes until tender.

2. Using a slotted spoon, transfer broccoli to a food processor (reserve the cooking liquid for thinning). Process until completely smooth and no fibrous material remains. Add a little of the reserved water if needed to achieve a smooth consistency. Serve warm.

CAULIFLOWER PURÉE

Pick a fresh cauliflower that has no signs of brown spots, flowers, or a slightly dingy color; those are all signs of one that's near the end of its shelf life. Cauliflower will stay fresh for up to 1 week in the refrigerator, but turn it on its "head" to prevent mold from settling in from excess moisture. Cauliflower contains lots of antioxidants that help protect against cancer.

Yields 15 servings

1 cup water

1 medium head cauliflower, trimmed and cut into florets

1. In a medium saucepan over medium-high heat, add water and bring to a boil. Add cauliflower to a steamer insert and set into saucepan. Cover and steam about 10 minutes until tender.

2. Using a slotted spoon, transfer cauliflower to a food processor (reserve the cooking liquid for thinning). Process until completely smooth and no fibrous material remains. Add a little of the reserved water if needed to achieve desired consistency. Serve warm.

SAVE THE STEM

Toss the leftover cauliflower stem, including any leaves, into your vegetable stock to give it extra flavor. Remove it along with all the other vegetables when the stock is done. No point in letting it go to waste!

SQUASH PURÉE

Butternut and acorn squash can be purchased year-round, but the best prices on these are in the fall. Use them to decorate your kitchen or dining table before you are ready to cook them. However, be sure to freeze the purée right away if you have any leftovers. Squash has a short shelf life once it's cooked and only lasts a few days in the refrigerator.

Yields 8 servings

1 medium butternut or acorn squash, halved and seeded

1. Preheat oven to 350°F.

2. Place cut squash skin-side down on a baking sheet. Bake 30 minutes until flesh is tender.

3. Scoop out squash into a food processor. Process until smooth, adding water a little at a time if needed to thin. Serve warm.

USING A FORK TO MASH

Depending on your baby's development, you may be able to skip puréeing using an electrical appliance altogether and simply mash baked squash with a fork. Some babies can handle slightly thicker textures at this age, and some are even able to go for it themselves using their hands. The same holds true for many other fruits and vegetables that don't include skins or thick stems that need more processing power. A fork will be your BFF.

PUMPKIN PURÉE

Canned pumpkin is available year-round, and is quick and easy to serve—just open the can. Make sure to buy pure pumpkin with no added spices, sugars, or dairy products. The rich orange color of the pumpkin tells you that it contains lots of beta-carotene! Pumpkin is also rich in potassium.

Yields 4 servings

½ (15-ounce) can pure pumpkin

1. In a small saucepan over medium heat, warm pumpkin.

2. Add water to thin if needed and simmer an additional 3 minutes. Remove and allow to cool slightly. Serve warm or chilled.

APRICOT PURÉE

Dried apricots will also work for this recipe. However, fresh is the best. Simmer dried apricots on the stove in a pot of water 8–10 minutes until tender and then purée.

Yields 10 servings

5 medium apricots
8 cups water

1. With a small paring knife, score a cross on the bottom of each apricot. This will make peeling easier.

2. In a medium saucepan over medium-high heat, bring water to a boil. Submerge apricots in boiling water for 1 minute. If the water is not covering the apricots, add more until they are completely submerged. Remove from heat and, leaving apricots in the pan, allow to cool to room temperature.

3. Starting from the cut, peel the skin away from the fruit and pull the flesh away from the pit. Discard the peel and pits.

4. Transfer apricots to a food processor. Process until smooth. Add water a little at a time to achieve desired consistency. Serve warm or chilled.

MANGO PURÉE

Mangoes are the sweetest in the summer, but they are still delicious other times of year as well. Mangoes contain a lot of antioxidants, including vitamins C, E, K, and beta-carotene, as well as minerals.

2 cups fresh or thawed frozen mango chunks

Add mango to a food processor. Process until smooth. Add water a little at a time to achieve desired consistency. Serve immediately.

PAPAYA PURÉE

Yields 15 servings

Pick a papaya that has a red-orange color, as a green papaya is usually not ripe. To ripen a green papaya, you can place it inside a paper bag along with a ripe banana to speed things along. Store the papaya on the countertop at room temperature until ready to use.

1 medium papaya, peeled and pitted

Add papaya to a food processor. Process until smooth. Add water a little at a time to achieve desired consistency. Serve immediately.

MAKE POPSICLES FROM PAPAYA

Fill the popsicle mold of your choice with puréed papaya and freeze up to 6 months. Pop out of the molds and give them to your baby and everyone else in the family for a super healthy dessert.

CHICKPEA PURÉE

Canned chickpeas with no salt added make this a very quick and easy purée. Keep a few cans on hand for mixing with other purées to make hummus, or to keep in your emergency stash. Chickpeas are also known as garbanzo beans. They create a wonderfully creamy texture and are a good source of protein, iron, fiber, zinc, and folate.

Yields 2-3 servings

½ cup canned chickpeas, drained and rinsed

Add chickpeas to a food processor. Process until smooth. Add water a little at a time if needed to achieve desired consistency. Serve immediately.

CANTALOUPE PURÉE

Sweet cantaloupe is extremely tasty and refreshing during the spring and summer months. It does not need to be cooked, making it easy to purée some for baby while you're cutting a wedge of it for yourself. Its runny consistency makes it good as a first food and is great when mixed with oatmeal or barley cereal.

Yields 10 servings

2 cups chopped cantaloupe

Add cantaloupe to a food processor. Process until smooth. Add water a little at a time to achieve desired consistency. Serve immediately.

CANTALOUPE-PEACH CHILLOUT FOR PARENTS

Here's an idea for parents: Blend 2 cups chopped cantaloupe, 1 cup fresh or frozen peaches, and the juice of 1 freshly squeezed lemon. Add stevia or honey to taste, if desired. Garnish with a few slices of fresh peach and enjoy!

CARROT PURÉE

Some vegetables, including carrots, may leak nitrates into the cooking water as they're boiled. For this reason, only make this purée for your baby if she is at least 7 months old. As an extra precaution, do not use the cooking water when thinning out this purée; use filtered water instead.

Yields 10 servings

1 cup water

2 pounds carrots, peeled and cut into chunks

1. In a medium saucepan over medium-high heat, add water and bring to a boil. Add carrots to a steamer insert and set into saucepan. Cover and steam about 10 minutes until tender.

2. Using a slotted spoon, transfer carrots to a food processor. Process until smooth. Add a little water if needed to achieve desired consistency. Serve warm.

CUCUMBER-MELON MASHUP
(PICTURED)

Cucumber and melon not only smell great together; they also taste great together, especially when you add a little mint. This is an instant purée because you do not need to cook the melon or cucumber. There is a little preparation, but once the seeds and skins are removed, it's smooth sailing.

Yields 4 servings

1 cup chopped honeydew melon

1 medium English cucumber, peeled and chopped

1 teaspoon chopped fresh mint

Add all ingredients to a food processor. Process until smooth. Serve chilled.

PLUM-BASIL PURÉE

Plums are incredibly high in vitamin C, which makes them a perfect pairing with another food rich in iron, like chickpeas! With this meal, your baby will benefit from protein, vitamin C, fiber, and other antioxidants. There are so many varieties of plums to choose from. Choose one that's locally grown in your area with a little sweetness.

Yields 8 servings

3 large sweet plums
5 cups water
1 tablespoon chopped fresh basil
¼ cup Chickpea Purée (see recipe in this chapter)

1. With a small paring knife, score a cross on the bottom of each plum. This will make peeling easier.

2. In a medium saucepan over medium-high heat, bring water to a boil. Submerge plums into boiling water for 1 minute until tender. If the water isn't covering the plums, add more until they are completely submerged. Remove from heat and, leaving plums in the pan, allow to cool to room temperature.

3. Starting from the cut, peel the skin away from the plum and pull the flesh away from the pit. Discard the peel and pits.

4. Transfer plums to a food processor. Add the basil. Process until smooth. Add water a little at a time to achieve desired consistency. Transfer to a large bowl.

5. To prepare a serving, in a small bowl, swirl together 2 tablespoons Plum-Basil Purée and 1 tablespoon Chickpea Purée. Serve warm.

PUMPKIN-PARSNIP PURÉE

Parsnips may be hard to find in some local grocery stores. Try looking for parsnips at the farmers' market or other markets that specialize in fresh produce. Parsnips look very similar to carrots, but they have a totally different taste that many babies love. They contain calcium, iron, zinc, and B vitamins.

Yields 2 servings

1 cup water

4 small parsnips

½ cup canned pure pumpkin

1. In a medium saucepan over medium-high heat, bring water to a boil. Add parsnips to a steamer insert and set into saucepan. Cover and steam about 10 minutes until tender.

2. Using a slotted spoon, transfer parsnips to a food processor (reserve the cooking liquid for thinning). Process until smooth. Add a little of the reserved water if needed to achieve desired consistency.

3. In a medium bowl, swirl parsnip purée and pumpkin together. Serve warm.

QUINOA MEDLEY

Time to break out the Homemade Quinoa Cereal and reap the nutritious benefits. When combined with pear and pumpkin, it makes a hearty dish containing protein, fiber, iron, vitamin C, and the list goes on. Serve it warm for a comforting meal.

Yields 2 servings

¼ cup Homemade Quinoa Cereal (see recipe in this chapter)

2 tablespoons canned pure pumpkin

2 tablespoons Pear Purée (see recipe in this chapter)

⅛ teaspoon ground cinnamon

1 teaspoon plant-based butter

In a small microwave-safe bowl, combine all ingredients. Microwave on 50 percent power 1 minute. Serve warm.

PEACHY MANGO RICE CEREAL

These two fruits are a combination that babies enjoy, especially with organic brown rice. Feel free to substitute any other homemade cereal mentioned in this chapter for the rice cereal.

Yields 1 serving

¼ cup Homemade Brown Rice Cereal (see recipe in this chapter)

2 tablespoons Mango Purée (see recipe in this chapter)

2 tablespoons Peach Purée (see recipe in this chapter)

1 teaspoon plant-based butter

In a small microwave-safe bowl, combine all ingredients. Microwave on 50 percent power 1 minute. Serve warm.

EDAMAME PURÉE

Edamame is a legume also known as soybeans. You can find organic shelled edamame in the freezer section of most grocery stores. Edamame is a great source of protein and has fiber, calcium, and iron.

Yields 4 servings

1 cup water
1 cup shelled edamame

1. In a medium saucepan over medium-high heat, bring water to a boil. Add edamame and cook 5 minutes.

2. Drain edamame and rinse with cool water; transfer to a food processor.

3. Process until mixture is a smooth purée. If needed, add additional water or vegetable stock to achieve desired consistency. Serve immediately.

IS EDAMAME ALLERGENIC?

Edamame is considered an allergenic food. However, current research shows that introducing babies to some allergenic foods early can actually prevent food allergies later on. It is always best to consult with your pediatrician when introducing new foods to your baby.

BANANA-OATMEAL MASH

Bananas pair very well with oatmeal cereal. This is sure to be a hit with your baby. Remember that bananas tend to constipate, so make sure you offer meals with apples, pears, or prunes to help prevent it.

Yields 1 serving

2 tablespoons Homemade Oatmeal Cereal (see recipe in this chapter)

2 tablespoons mashed banana

In a small bowl, combine all ingredients. Serve immediately.

PAPAYA-PEAR OATMEAL

This fruity, delicious oatmeal is healthy for baby, and it's a unique combination you won't find on the shelf—only in your kitchen.

Yields 2 servings

¼ cup Homemade Oatmeal Cereal (see recipe in this chapter)

2 tablespoons Papaya Purée (see recipe in this chapter)

2 tablespoons Pear Purée (see recipe in this chapter)

In a small bowl, combine all ingredients. Serve immediately.

APPLE-PAPAYA PORRIDGE

This combination is a sweet and yummy way to start the day with the protein and heartiness that quinoa cereal provides. Even though at this stage the quinoa is served more on the watery side, it still provides the same nutrition as fully cooked quinoa. The addition of apple and papaya makes this purée sweet and super tasty.

Yields 2 servings

¼ cup Homemade Quinoa Cereal (see recipe in this chapter)

2 tablespoons Papaya Purée (see recipe in this chapter)

2 tablespoons Apple Purée (see recipe in this chapter)

In a small bowl, combine all ingredients. Serve immediately.

BANANA-APRICOT OATMEAL

This combination includes many of the nutrients that a growing baby needs, including potassium, iron, and vitamin A.

Yields 2 servings

¼ cup Homemade Oatmeal Cereal (see recipe in this chapter)

2 tablespoons mashed banana

2 tablespoons Apricot Purée (see recipe in this chapter)

In a small bowl, combine all ingredients. Serve immediately.

BACK TO THE BASICS

Remember if you don't have any basic purées in your freezer stash, you can always go back to the basics discussed earlier in this chapter to make fresh, single-ingredient purées for combinations. Also, be creative and use what you have on hand, and substitute when necessary. The best thing about homemade food is you can mix and match and have fun!

PEACHY PUMPKIN OATMEAL

The combination of pumpkin and peach results in a vibrant orange color and subtly sweet flavor that no baby can resist. But what's better is that you're serving your baby a meal packed with lots of iron and fiber. It's a win-win!

Yields 2 servings

¼ cup Homemade Oatmeal Cereal (see recipe in this chapter)

2 tablespoons canned pure pumpkin

2 tablespoons Peach Purée (see recipe in this chapter)

In a small bowl, combine all ingredients. Serve immediately.

FRUITY AVOCADO QUINOA CEREAL

Avocados and bananas will turn brown after sitting out for a while, so serve this purée immediately after preparation. The bananas and pears will add a little more flavor, resulting in a purée that is less tart and more nutritious! This dish is a good source of healthy monounsaturated fat, iron, potassium, and other nutrients.

Yields 2 servings

2 tablespoons Homemade Quinoa Cereal (see recipe in this chapter)

2 tablespoons mashed avocado

1 tablespoon mashed banana

1 tablespoon Pear Purée (see recipe in this chapter)

In a small bowl, combine all ingredients. Serve immediately.

AVOCADO FACTS

Avocados were introduced to the United States from Mexico in the nineteenth century. Ninety-five percent of avocado production is cultivated in California. Avocados are good sources of monounsaturated fats, which aid in brain and visual development for your baby.

PRUNE-BARLEY BOWEL HELPER

This is a great recipe to use if your baby feels constipated. The high fiber content in barley and prunes can help move things along. Make sure you're giving your baby plenty of breast milk with fiber-rich foods.

Yields 1 serving

2 tablespoons Homemade Barley Cereal (see recipe in this chapter)

2 tablespoons Prune Purée (see recipe in this chapter)

In a small bowl, combine all ingredients. Serve immediately.

APPLE, PUMPKIN, AND QUINOA BONANZA

The creaminess of the pumpkin adds a rich taste and smooth texture to this dish that your baby will fall in love with. When paired with apple and banana, it's a nutrient powerhouse!

Yields 4 servings

2 tablespoons Homemade Quinoa Cereal (see recipe in this chapter)

2 tablespoons Apple Purée (see recipe in this chapter)

2 tablespoons canned pure pumpkin

1 tablespoon mashed banana

In a small bowl, combine all ingredients. Serve immediately.

ORGANIC STORE-BOUGHT APPLESAUCE

Keep a jar or two of organic applesauce on hand for those moments when you need food in a pinch. Make sure the applesauce has no added sugar or other ingredients. It can be mixed in with frozen purées, vegetables, or served by itself.

APPLE-PLUM QUINOA CEREAL

This is a great way to use apples or plums that are ever so slightly past their prime and no longer ideal for eating whole. You can also freeze this superfood purée, so why not make a big batch?

Yields 2 servings

¼ cup Homemade Quinoa Cereal (see recipe in this chapter)

2 tablespoons Apple Purée (see recipe in this chapter)

2 tablespoons Plum Purée (see recipe in this chapter)

⅛ teaspoon ground cinnamon

In a small bowl, combine all ingredients. Serve immediately.

AVOCADO-BANANA MASH

Keep a fresh banana and avocado in your baby's lunch bag to make an instant purée while on the run. Both these fruits come in their own convenient packaging, so they are perfect to take on the go!

Yields 1 serving

2 tablespoons mashed avocado

2 tablespoons mashed banana

In a small bowl, combine all ingredients and mash together with a fork until desired consistency is achieved. Serve immediately.

RIPEN THOSE BANANAS

If your bananas are a little green when you purchase them, place them in a brown bag and allow them to ripen undisturbed. Check them the next day, and you'll discover your bananas have ripened!

BANANA-BLUEBERRY BUCKLE
(PICTURED)

Experts say to eat a handful of blueberries each day for good health. While you're making this dish for baby, make a banana-blueberry buckle smoothie with 100 percent grape juice for a powerful antioxidant boost for yourself!

Yields 4 servings

¼ cup blueberries

1 large ripe banana, peeled

1 teaspoon fresh lemon juice

Add all ingredients to a food processor. Purée until smooth. Serve immediately.

PLUM-PEAR YOGURT

Using plant-based yogurt such as oat milk is a great way to reap the probiotic benefits of this healthy purée. Oat milk is made from oats, making it one of the safest plant-based yogurts that doesn't come from a nut source. You can also substitute coconut yogurt, since coconut allergies are rare, but check with your pediatrician to get the thumbs-up before introducing coconut yogurt. Remaining portions will keep in the refrigerator up to 4 days.

Yields 2 servings

2 tablespoons Plum Purée (see recipe in this chapter)

2 tablespoons Pear Purée (see recipe in this chapter)

2 tablespoons plain oat milk yogurt alternative

In a small bowl, combine all ingredients. Serve immediately.

AVOCADO-PUMPKIN MASH

When making this recipe, swirl the pumpkin purée into the mashed avocado with a knife for a dazzling presentation.

2 tablespoons mashed avocado
2 tablespoons canned pure pumpkin

In a small bowl, combine all ingredients. Serve immediately.

APRICOT-PEAR PURÉE

If your baby is having trouble with bowel movements, this is a great purée to turn to—pears are filled with fiber and can be used to help alleviate constipation.

2 tablespoons Apricot Purée (see recipe in this chapter)
2 tablespoons Pear Purée (see recipe in this chapter)

In a small bowl, combine all ingredients. Serve immediately.

MANGO-PEAR PURÉE

Give your baby a tiny taste of the tropics with this purée, which features mango paired with pear (for extra fiber)! Make a bunch in advance and freeze for a ray of sunshine on a rainy day.

Yields 1 serving

2 tablespoons Mango Purée (see recipe in this chapter)

2 tablespoons Pear Purée (see recipe in this chapter)

In a small bowl, combine all ingredients. Serve immediately.

MANGO-BANANA MASHUP

While you're making this sweet purée for baby, reserve some of the remaining fruit for yourself. Then, simply cut bananas and mangoes into small chunks and add on top of your favorite plant-based cereal. The freshness of the fruit combined with the cereal will perk you up in the morning!

Yields 1 serving

2 tablespoons mashed banana

2 tablespoons Mango Purée (see recipe in this chapter)

In a small bowl, combine all ingredients. Serve immediately.

PAPAYA AND BANANA BLEND

Papaya and bananas are an interesting blend that some babies don't expect because papayas are not the most common baby food, but they should be. Papayas are an exotic fruit, but they have anti-inflammatory properties that make them wonderful additions to your meal rotation to help ward off viruses and other infections.

Yields I serving

2 tablespoons Papaya Purée (see recipe in this chapter)

2 tablespoons mashed banana

⅛ teaspoon ground cinnamon

In a small bowl, combine all ingredients. Serve immediately.

GREEN BEANS AND QUINOA COMBO
(PICTURED)

You can dial up the flavor on recipes once your baby has mastered all the single-ingredient foods. Adding flavorful herbs and spices like those in this recipe makes eating vegetables enjoyable and interesting!

Yields I serving

2 tablespoons Homemade Quinoa Cereal (see recipe in this chapter)

2 tablespoons Green Bean Purée (see recipe in this chapter)

⅛ teaspoon onion powder

½ teaspoon plant-based butter

In a small bowl, combine all ingredients. Serve immediately.

JUST PEACHY PEAR PURÉE

Ignite your baby's senses with this refreshing combination. The peaches and pears can be puréed raw once your baby is an established purée connoisseur.

Yields 1 serving

2 tablespoons Peach Purée **(see recipe in this chapter)**
2 tablespoons Pear Purée **(see recipe in this chapter)**
1 tablespoon oat milk yogurt alternative
1 teaspoon ground cinnamon

In a small bowl, combine all ingredients. Serve chilled.

PEACH-AVOCADO SMASH

Here's a wonderful purée to make when summer peaches are in season! For an unforgettable experience, visit a pick-your-own farm and pluck your very own fresh, organic peaches off the tree.

Yields 1 serving

2 tablespoons Peach Purée **(see recipe in this chapter)**
2 tablespoons mashed avocado

In a small bowl, combine all ingredients. Serve immediately.

ARE UNUSUAL COMBINATIONS TASTY FOR BABY?

Because babies are developing taste buds, it's okay to try unconventional combinations of fruits and vegetables, even if they don't seem like they would taste good together. Your child may love an offbeat mixture of plums and sweet peas. Experimenting is fun, and you may learn a thing or two about new food combos your baby actually enjoys.

PEACHY BROWN RICE PURÉE

When peaches and nectarines are in season, there's nothing more decadent. This sweet, smooth cereal gives your baby a taste of the delicious foods she'll enjoy as she grows up eating your wholesome meals. Peaches and nectarines are similar, but they taste slightly different.

Yields 1 serving

2 tablespoons Homemade Brown Rice Cereal (see recipe in this chapter)

2 tablespoons Peach Purée (see recipe in this chapter)

2 tablespoons Nectarine Purée (see recipe in this chapter)

In a small bowl, combine all ingredients. Serve immediately.

BANANA-PUMPKIN PLEASER

Not only is this a good combination served alone; you can also use this flavorful purée as a spread on toast or teething biscuits when teething starts at around 8 or 9 months.

Yields 1 serving

2 tablespoons mashed banana

2 tablespoons canned pure pumpkin

In a small bowl, combine all ingredients. Serve immediately.

BLISSFUL GREENS

This delicious combo is especially healthy for baby, providing a nice dose of healthy fat, vitamin K, vitamin C, potassium, and iron.

Yields I serving

2 tablespoons Green Bean Purée (see recipe in this chapter)
2 tablespoons mashed avocado

In a small bowl, combine all ingredients. Serve immediately.

CARROT-APPLE PURÉE

You don't have to stick with orange carrots—there are many varieties to choose from. You may not find them at your local grocery, but the local farmers' market or CSA may have colors on hand like yellow, red, or purple. When you can get hold of those rare varieties, stock up and freeze.

Yields 4 servings

1 cup water
1 medium carrot, peeled and cut into chunks
½ cup Apple Purée

1. In a medium saucepan over medium-high heat, add water and bring to a boil. Add carrot to a steamer insert and set into saucepan. Cover and steam about 10 minutes until tender.

2. Using a slotted spoon, transfer carrot to a food processor. Process until smooth.

3. In a small bowl, combine carrot purée and Apple Purée. Serve warm or chilled.

HOLD ON, HONEY!

Remember to hold off on honey until your baby is at least 12 months old. For babies younger than 12 months, eating honey can cause a life-threatening illness called infant botulism. Your baby does not need any added sweeteners at this age, but if you must use sweetener, consider using puréed dates or bananas to sweeten foods naturally without any added sugar.

BRIGHT ZUCCHINI AND BROWN RICE

Zucchini squash comes in vibrant hues of green and yellow. Experiment with different colors for a colorful meal your baby will enjoy.

Yields 2 servings

2 tablespoons Zucchini Purée (see recipe in this chapter)

2 tablespoons Homemade Brown Rice Cereal (see recipe in this chapter)

In a small bowl, combine all ingredients. Serve immediately.

ENCHANTING APPLE SURPRISE

A pleasant surprise awaits your baby, who will savor the sweetness in this seasonal pairing. This combination boasts vitamin C and antioxidants, and it supports healthy digestion.

Yields 2 servings

2 tablespoons Apple Purée (see recipe in this chapter)

1 tablespoon Pear Purée (see recipe in this chapter)

1 tablespoon Zucchini Purée (see recipe in this chapter)

⅛ teaspoon ground allspice

In a small bowl, combine all ingredients. Serve immediately.

CARROT–SWEET POTATO PURÉE

This flavorful—and vibrant!—dish is nutritiously rich with antioxidants.

Yields 2 servings

2 tablespoons Carrot Purée (see recipe in this chapter)

2 tablespoons Sweet Potato Purée (see recipe in this chapter)

In a small bowl, combine all ingredients. Serve immediately.

SWEET PEA TANGO

(PICTURED)

Mangoes and sweet peas tango in perfect harmony in this purée. When you find mangoes on sale, buy a bunch and make batches to freeze!

Yields 2 servings

2 tablespoons Sweet Pea Purée (see recipe in this chapter)

2 tablespoons Mango Purée (see recipe in this chapter)

In a small bowl, combine all ingredients. Serve immediately.

ISLAND BREAKFAST CEREAL

Bring the islands to your purée masterpieces by using frozen fruit in winter when local options are scarce. Mangoes and papayas are high in vitamin C, which makes iron absorption easier. This would be a great purée to accompany other iron-rich foods.

Yields 4 servings

¼ cup Homemade Brown Rice Cereal
(see recipe in this chapter)
2 tablespoons Papaya Purée
(see recipe in this chapter)
2 tablespoons Mango Purée
(see recipe in this chapter)

In a small bowl, combine all ingredients. Serve immediately.

BANANA AND APRICOT PURÉE

Make sure the apricots are sweet when you're ready to make this recipe. If apricots aren't in season or aren't quite ripe yet, you can substitute dried apricots.

Yields 2 servings

2 tablespoons Apricot Purée
(see recipe in this chapter)
2 tablespoons mashed banana

In a small bowl, combine all ingredients. Serve immediately.

APPLE-APRICOT PURÉE

Feeding this yummy purée to your baby can also become a fun way to introduce some words (apple, apricot) to your little one—lunchtime, brought to you by the letter A!

Yields 1 serving

2 tablespoons Apple Purée
(see recipe in this chapter)

2 tablespoons Apricot Purée
(see recipe in this chapter)

In a small bowl, combine all ingredients. Serve immediately.

PRUNE, APRICOT, AND YOGURT BLEND

This is the perfect creamy, sweet combo to serve to your constipated little one. Prunes help move baby's bowels, and the yogurt soothes the digestive track with all sorts of good bacteria.

Yields 3 servings

2 tablespoons oat milk yogurt alternative

2 tablespoons Apricot Purée
(see recipe in this chapter)

2 tablespoons Prune Purée
(see recipe in this chapter)

In a small bowl, combine all ingredients. Serve immediately.

SQUASH, APPLE, AND PEAR MEDLEY

(PICTURED)

If you aren't able to find butternut squash at your local grocery or farmers' market, feel free to use another variety of winter squash—or even sweet potato!—for this recipe.

Yields 6 servings

½ cup peeled butternut squash chunks
¼ cup water
½ cup coarsely chopped apple
½ cup coarsely chopped pear

1. In a medium saucepan over medium-high heat, combine all ingredients. Bring to a boil, stirring frequently, and cook 8–10 minutes until fork-tender.

2. Using a slotted spoon, transfer squash, pear, and apple to a food processor. Process until smooth. Add water a little at a time if needed to achieve desired consistency. Serve warm or chilled.

APPLE-BANANA OATMEAL

Most babies prefer the taste of sweet apples over tart apples, so it's best to stay away from Granny Smith apples when making apple purées for the earliest eaters.

Yields 3 servings

2 tablespoons Homemade Oatmeal Cereal (see recipe in this chapter)
2 tablespoons Apple Purée (see recipe in this chapter)
2 tablespoons mashed banana

In a small bowl, combine all ingredients. Serve immediately.

PLUMMY POTATOES

The variety of potatoes available at the market can sometimes be mind-boggling. For this recipe, note that white russet or butter gold potatoes work best.

Yields 2 servings

1 medium Yukon Gold potato, **peeled and cut into small chunks**

1 medium ripe plum, peeled, pitted, and cut into chunks

1. In a small saucepan over medium heat, combine potato and just enough water to cover. Bring to a boil and cook 10–15 minutes until fork-tender.

2. Combine plum and cooked potato in a blender. Pulse until smooth. Thin with water or plant milk if needed to achieve desired consistency. Serve warm.

BUTTERNUT SQUASH PLUS CARROT PURÉE

Take advantage of autumn, when both of these vegetables are in season. Don't forget to freeze any leftovers to enjoy in the spring!

Yields 2 servings

2 tablespoons Squash Purée (see recipe in this chapter)

2 tablespoons Carrot Purée (see recipe in this chapter)

In a small bowl, combine all ingredients. Serve immediately.

FALL PUMPKIN YOGURT

When the trees are starting to change colors and fall is settling in, make this delicious recipe to celebrate the new season.

Yields 8 servings

2 tablespoons canned pure pumpkin or Pumpkin Purée (see recipe in this chapter)

2 tablespoons oat milk yogurt alternative

In a small bowl, combine all ingredients. Serve immediately.

PEAR AND PEACH PURÉE

Both pears and peaches are known to aid in digestion and keep things running efficiently. This purée also pairs well with cereal.

Yields 2 servings

2 tablespoons Pear Purée **(see recipe in this chapter)**

2 tablespoons Peach Purée **(see recipe in this chapter)**

In a small bowl, combine all ingredients. Serve immediately.

APPLE-PEAR BARLEY CEREAL

A good source of vitamin A, folate, and even protein, barley packs a nutritional punch! Pair it with the sweet goodness of apples and pears, and you've got a well-rounded meal for your little one.

2 tablespoons Homemade Barley Cereal
(see recipe in this chapter)
2 tablespoons Apple Purée
(see recipe in this chapter)
2 tablespoons Pear Purée
(see recipe in this chapter)

In a small bowl, combine all ingredients. Serve immediately.

VEGETABLE STOCK

Vegetable stock is great to use in place of water to add extra flavor to purées. Anytime water is called for in a recipe and you have vegetable stock on hand, feel free to substitute. This also makes a great base for any type of soup.

2 teaspoons extra-virgin olive oil
1 small yellow onion, peeled and chopped
4 cloves garlic, peeled and minced
1 medium stalk celery with leafy top, chopped
1 large carrot, peeled and chopped
3 medium green onions, trimmed and sliced
1 bay leaf
4 sprigs fresh flat-leaf parsley
2 sprigs fresh thyme
4 cups cold water

1. In a large stockpot over medium-high heat, heat oil. Add all vegetables and herbs. Cook 5 minutes, stirring frequently.

2. Add water and bring to a boil. Reduce heat to low and simmer uncovered 45 minutes.

3. Remove from heat and allow to cool about 1 hour. Strain and discard vegetables.

4. Store stock in a large, tightly covered jar in the refrigerator up to 4 days until ready to serve, or freeze in a freezer-safe container up to 1 month.

ZUCCHINI AND CARROT PURÉE

This purée is rich in antioxidants such as lutein and beta-carotene along with a long list of vitamins and minerals. All the many different varieties of carrots and zucchini have an abundance of nutrition and beauty. Give them all a try!

Yields 2 servings

2 tablespoons Carrot Purée
(see recipe in this chapter)
2 tablespoons Zucchini Purée
(see recipe in this chapter)

In a small bowl, combine all ingredients. Serve immediately.

TROPICAL PAPAYA COCONUT

This recipe is a favorite among babies due to the richness and healthy fats the coconut milk provides. Use canned coconut to reap the nutritional benefits of the healthy monounsaturated fat. Make sure to shake up the can to evenly distribute the cream that rises to the top. However, if you have the carton variety, feel free to substitute!

Yields 2 servings

¼ cup Papaya Purée
(see recipe in this chapter)
2 tablespoons unsweetened canned coconut milk, plus more for thinning
2 tablespoons Homemade Brown Rice Cereal (see recipe in this chapter)

In a small bowl, combine all ingredients. Thin with more milk if desired. Serve immediately.

5

MORE FLAVOR TO SAVOR:
INTRODUCING SEMI-SMOOTH PURÉES
######## (8-9 MONTHS) ########

It's time for your little explorer to become more adventurous in trying new flavors, textures, and even more herbs and spices! From the time your child is eight months old, start puréeing her meal to a semi-smooth consistency to allow your baby plenty of chewing practice. You may even notice a tooth or two popping through! Breast milk is still a very important part of your child's diet, so make sure she is getting 24–40 ounces of breast milk or iron-fortified plant-based formula per day.

You may continue serving all of the meals in Chapter 4, and you will find that you will be able to mix and match those basic purées with new foods such as lentils, pasta, tofu, and small amounts of citrus. Because citrus can cause an adverse reaction in babies younger than 12 months, check with your pediatrician if your baby is sensitive to acidic foods, especially if serving citrus foods, like orange segments, alone. Some of the recipes in this chapter introduce hints of citrus in purées, so it's important to get the thumbs-up before making them. Continue serving grain cereals and about ¼–½ cup of fruits and vegetables per day. If her pincer grasp is ready, offer her finger foods such as soft crackers, toast, cereal Os, or teething biscuits.

Babies do not need juice at all, and because of its high levels of sugar, it is strongly discouraged as a beverage. Plain water or fruit-infused water are better choices. If you must give juice, do so sparingly, limiting it to 2 ounces per day, and dilute it with 50 percent filtered water. Also, make sure it's 100 percent organic fruit juice with no added sugar.

GINGERED APPLE AND PLUM COMPOTE

Golden Delicious, Fuji, or Pink Lady apples make the best choices for this compote, as they are sweeter than other varieties.

Yields 8 servings

1 medium sweet apple, peeled, cored, and coarsely chopped

2 small plums, peeled, pitted, and coarsely chopped

⅛ teaspoon ground cinnamon

⅛ teaspoon ground ginger

¼ cup water

1. In a medium saucepan over medium heat, combine all ingredients. Cover and cook about 10 minutes until apple is very tender and starts to break apart. Remove from heat and cool slightly.

2. Mash with a potato masher or the back of a spoon. The mixture should have small chunks intact, similar to fruit preserves. Transfer to a blender or food processor if a finer consistency is needed. Serve warm.

APPLESAUCE À LA RASPBERRY

Fresh raspberry applesauce beats any store-bought version if you can even find it. Make extra, as everyone will enjoy this unique take on applesauce. If you don't have vanilla bean paste on hand, you can use ¼ teaspoon vanilla extract.

Yields 4 servings

1 medium apple, peeled, cored, and coarsely chopped

½ cup fresh raspberries

⅛ teaspoon ground cinnamon

⅛ teaspoon pure vanilla bean paste

¼ cup water

1. In a medium saucepan over medium-low heat, combine apple, raspberries, cinnamon, vanilla bean paste, and water. Cover and simmer about 15 minutes until apple is completely cooked and fork-tender. Remove from heat and let stand 5 minutes.

2. Transfer to a food processor. Pulse until semi-smooth, allowing small chunks to remain, or continue to purée to achieve desired consistency. Add water or plant milk to thin as needed. Serve chilled.

MAPLE, APPLE, AND DATE PURÉE

Soft, plump dates make this purée a lot easier to process. This recipe requires a few hours of presoaking, so while you're waiting on that, make applesauce out of the remaining apples you have on hand. You can use this purée to naturally sweeten other purées or as a spread.

Yields 3 servings

¼ cup medium pitted dates

1 medium Granny Smith apple, peeled, cored, and quartered

¼ teaspoon ground cinnamon

¼ teaspoon natural maple extract

¼ cup water

1. Place dates in a medium bowl and cover with boiling water. Allow to soak 3–4 hours until they are completely hydrated.

2. In a medium saucepan over medium-low heat, combine apple cinnamon, maple extract, and water. Simmer 25 minutes until completely tender.

3. Drain apple pieces and combine with soaked dates in a food processor.

4. Pulse until mixture reaches a semi-smooth consistency. Add water to thin if needed. Serve immediately.

NATURAL BABY LAXATIVES

Just like adults, babies occasionally suffer from constipation. Dates, plums, prunes, and figs are among many foods that provide excellent relief. Offering these foods in the form of purées should do the job!

APRICOT JASMINE RICE

You can use previously frozen Apricot Purée (see recipe in Chapter 4) in this dish to make a quick meal for baby. However, remember not to refreeze previously frozen purées.

Yields 2 servings

¼ cup organic brown jasmine rice

½ cup water

1 teaspoon plant-based butter

⅛ teaspoon ground ginger

1 medium ripe apricot, peeled, pitted, and chopped

1. In a small saucepan over medium-high heat, combine rice with water and bring to a boil. Reduce heat to low, cover, and simmer 20 minutes until all liquid has been absorbed. Add butter and ginger. Stir to combine.

2. Transfer rice and apricot to a food processor. Pulse until a semi-smooth consistency is reached. Serve warm.

DO FRUITS HAVE TO BE PEELED?

Peeling fruit is a good idea for many reasons. Peeling ensures there is no pesticide residue on conventional fruits and also helps to prevent choking on any unprocessed skins from puréeing. As your baby gets older and is consistently enjoying a variety of fruits without any reactions, you can cook fruits with the peel intact.

FRUITY YOGURT PARFAIT
(PICTURED)

Instead of puréed fruits, your baby can now handle them cut into tiny pieces and added to purées. At this point, your baby may want to experiment with chewing and self-feeding, so give her a spoon and let her have some fun! If your baby is okay to have coconut yogurt, feel free to substitute that for a new flavor.

Yields 2 servings

¼ cup diced ripe banana, peach, or plum
½ cup oat milk yogurt alternative

1. Fork-mash your fruit of choice until smooth.

2. In a small bowl, layer yogurt, then fruit, then yogurt for a baby parfait. Serve immediately.

AVOCADO AND KIWI MASH

The kiwi in this recipe will add a boost of vitamins C and E to the avocado and an interesting taste. Pick a soft, plump kiwi to ensure it's ripe enough for baby.

Yields 4 servings

½ medium ripe kiwifruit, seeded and cored
1 (1") slice medium ripe avocado

Place kiwi and avocado slice on a plate. Mash together with a fork until semi-smooth. If needed, add a little water or plant-based milk for a creamier texture. Serve immediately.

BABY SUCCOTASH

Corn offers a sweet flavor that appeals to many babies. This dish adds lots of texture because of the corn kernel hulls. If the texture is too much, try offering this dish again in the third stage.

Yields 3 servings

½ cup frozen lima beans
½ cup frozen corn kernels
1 teaspoon plant-based butter
1 teaspoon diced yellow onion
2 cups water

1. In a medium saucepan over medium-high heat, combine all ingredients and bring to a boil. Reduce heat to low and simmer about 15 minutes until tender.

2. Transfer all ingredients to a food processor. Purée 30 seconds.

3. Thin with leftover cooking water as needed and purée until semi-smooth. Serve warm.

BANANA-APPLE FARINA

Expand your baby's horizons by trying this recipe using farina, a creamy wheat cereal that's great for breakfast.

Yields 4 servings

1 cup water
3 tablespoons farina
½ very ripe medium banana, peeled
½ cup Apple Purée (see recipe in Chapter 4)

1. In a small saucepan over medium-high heat, bring water to a boil. Add farina and stir well.

2. Reduce heat to low and cook 1–3 minutes until farina thickens, stirring continuously.

3. Remove from the heat and allow to cool about 10 minutes.

4. Remove any brown spots from banana and place in a small bowl. Fork-mash until creamy.

5. Stir Apple Purée and banana into cooled farina. Serve immediately.

BANANAS FOSTER FOR BABY

A traditional bananas foster recipe includes caramel sauce, rum, and brown sugar. This recipe is an all-natural remix suitable for baby.

Yields 1 serving

½ teaspoon plant-based butter
2 tablespoons unsweetened coconut flakes
⅛ teaspoon vanilla extract
½ small banana
½ teaspoon fresh lemon juice

1. In a small saucepan over medium heat, melt butter. Stir in coconut flakes and vanilla. Remove from heat.

2. In a small bowl, mash banana with fork and then drizzle with lemon juice.

3. Add coconut mixture to banana; stir together and serve.

BASIC BARLEY

This is not the same Homemade Barley Cereal from stage 1 that was ground into a powder (see recipe in Chapter 4). Your little one is growing and no longer needs a runny texture. This is the real-deal barley. This versatile, nutritious grain supports healthy brain development and offers baby a healthy dose of iron, phosphorous, magnesium, zinc, and potassium. Use this basic recipe to combine with other purées in this chapter to ensure your baby is getting enough of these essential nutrients.

Yields 7–8 servings

1 cup hulled barley, rinsed
3 cups plus 1 tablespoon water, divided

1. In a small saucepan over low heat, combine barley and 3 cups water. Cover and simmer 55 minutes until barley is tender. Transfer barley to a food processor with remaining 1 tablespoon water and pulse to combine. The texture should be broken up but not completely smooth.

2. Serve immediately or refrigerate up to 5 days until ready to use.

BLUEBERRY CREAM PIE

No dairy here! This recipe uses the goodness of oat milk yogurt for its creaminess. Coconut milk yogurt is another great option.

Yields 1 serving

¼ cup blueberries
1 tablespoon oat milk yogurt alternative

1. Purée blueberries in a blender to a smooth consistency. Push through sieve to remove any fibrous material, if necessary.

2. In a small bowl, combine blueberry purée and yogurt. Serve immediately.

BLUEBERRY APPLESAUCE

Blueberries add a deep, rich, velvety texture to this applesauce and deliver a boatload of antioxidants in every bite. The apple plays a healthy role too, adding vitamin C and fiber to make a harmonious dish.

Yields 3 servings

1 medium apple, peeled, cored, and cut into large chunks
½ cup blueberries
⅛ teaspoon vanilla extract
¼ cup water

1. In a medium saucepan over medium-low heat, combine all ingredients. Simmer about 25 minutes until apple and berries are completely tender.

2. Using a slotted spoon, transfer mixture to a blender. Purée until mixture is semi-smooth, adding more water if necessary to achieve desired consistency. Serve immediately.

BLUEBERRY AND VANILLA DREAM

Get two for one: Make an extra batch of this recipe and freeze it in festive ice cube tray molds, with shapes such as hearts or stars. Once the cubes are frozen, add them to sparkling lemonade or your favorite beverage for extra flavor and a powerful blend of antioxidants!

Yields 2 servings

1 cup blueberries
¼ cup water
¼ teaspoon vanilla extract

1. In a small saucepan over medium heat, combine all ingredients. Cook about 8 minutes until blueberries start to burst open.

2. Transfer mixture to a blender. Purée until smooth. Push through a fine-mesh strainer to remove any fibrous material if needed. Serve warm or chilled.

BLUEBERRY-POMEGRANATE PARFAIT

When blueberries come into season, stock up on them and freeze them whole. Enjoy them year-round in smoothies, pies, and recipes like this one.

Yields 1 serving

¼ cup blueberries
1 tablespoon pomegranate seeds
2 tablespoons plant-based vanilla yogurt

1. In a blender, purée blueberries and pomegranate seeds to a smooth consistency. Push through a fine-mesh strainer to remove any fibrous material if necessary.

2. Transfer mixture to a small bowl and fold in yogurt. Serve immediately.

POMEGRANATE-GLAZED CARROTS

(PICTURED)

This savory dish combines the sweetness from the carrots with the tartness of the pomegranate juice into a savory purée.

Yields 3 servings

1 cup chopped carrots
2 tablespoons 100 percent pomegranate juice

1. In a medium saucepan over medium-high heat, combine carrots with enough water to cover. Bring to a boil. Reduce heat to low and simmer 15–20 minutes until carrots are tender.

2. Drain carrots and transfer to a blender. Purée about 30 seconds. Add water to thin if necessary to achieve desired consistency. Continue puréeing until smooth.

3. In a small saucepan over medium-high heat, add pomegranate juice. Cook 15 minutes until juice is reduced by half.

4. In a medium bowl, combine juice and carrot purée. Serve warm.

CABBAGE PATCH PURÉE

Cabbage comes in many different varieties, including red, napa, savoy, and bok choy. For this recipe choose a traditional green cabbage with lots of big, green outer leaves. Make sure the cabbage is very tender before puréeing. For an even heartier dish, serve with Southern Lima Bean Purée (see recipe in this chapter).

Yields 10 servings

1 small head cabbage, cored and chopped
6 cups Vegetable Stock (see recipe in Chapter 4)
2 tablespoons plant-based butter
½ cup chopped yellow onion

1. In a large pot over medium-high heat, combine all ingredients. Bring to a boil.

2. Reduce heat to medium-low and simmer 30 minutes until cabbage is very tender, stirring occasionally.

3. Using a slotted spoon, transfer cabbage and onion to a blender. Purée to a smooth consistency. Serve warm.

BROCCOLI AND CAULIFLOWER WITH GARLIC

This flavorful, fiber-rich purée helps keep your baby's belly feeling satisfied. Serve with Homemade Brown Rice Cereal or Homemade Quinoa Cereal (see Chapter 4).

Yields 4–6 servings

1 cup water
½ cup broccoli florets
½ cup cauliflower florets
1 teaspoon plant-based butter, melted
¼ teaspoon minced garlic

1. In a medium saucepan over medium-high heat, add water and bring to a boil. Add broccoli and cauliflower to a steamer insert and set into saucepan. Cover and steam about 10 minutes until tender.

2. Using a slotted spoon, transfer broccoli and cauliflower to a food processor (reserve the cooking liquid for thinning). Add butter and garlic. Purée to a semi-smooth consistency. Add any remaining cooking liquid to thin as needed. Serve warm.

CINNAMON, APPLE, AND SWEET POTATO SURPRISE

The juices from baking the apple and sweet potato are complemented in this dish by the wonderful taste and aroma of cinnamon. The coconut oil adds healthy monounsaturated fat and a great flavor. If you don't have coconut oil, feel free to use plant-based butter instead.

Yields I serving

1 small apple, peeled, cored, and sliced
1 small sweet potato, peeled and cubed
¼ teaspoon ground cinnamon
⅛ teaspoon ground nutmeg
1 teaspoon extra-virgin coconut oil

1. Preheat oven to 350°F.

2. In an 8" × 8" square dish, toss together apple, sweet potato, cinnamon, nutmeg, and coconut oil.

3. Bake 40 minutes until apple and sweet potato are tender.

4. Transfer to a blender with liquid and purée or fork-mash. Add water if needed to thin. Serve warm.

DILL CARROTS WITH QUINOA

Using quinoa in recipes will provide your baby with an excellent source of protein and the essential amino acids he needs. It is a perfect choice to blend in with other vegetables because it's easy to digest and really kicks up the nutrition of the meal.

Yields 3 servings

½ cup coarsely chopped carrot
2 tablespoons quinoa, rinsed
1 teaspoon dried dill
½ teaspoon plant-based butter

1. In a medium saucepan over medium-high heat, combine all ingredients and add just enough water to cover. Bring to a boil.

2. Reduce heat to low, cover, and simmer about 20 minutes until most of the water is absorbed.

3. Transfer mixture into a food processor. Pulse until semi-smooth. Add more water if necessary to thin. Serve immediately.

CHICKPEA, CARROT, AND CAULIFLOWER MASH

Remember that chickpeas are also called garbanzo beans, so if you don't see "chickpeas" at the store, look f,or "garbanzo beans" in the canned food aisle. You can also purchase dried beans and follow the instructions on the package for preparing. Serve this purée with quinoa.

Yields 8 servings

1 cup water
2 medium carrots, peeled and sliced
1 cup cauliflower florets
2 cups canned chickpeas, drained and rinsed

1. In a medium saucepan over medium-high heat, add water and bring to a boil. Add carrots and cauliflower to a steamer insert and set into saucepan. Cover and steam about 6 minutes until very tender.

2. In a medium bowl, combine steamed vegetables with chickpeas and mash with a potato masher or fork.

3. Add water as necessary to reach a semi-smooth consistency. Serve warm.

CAULIFLOWER CASSEROLE

Nutritional yeast adds a "cheesy" flavor to plant-based meals without dairy, and it has an abundance of nutrition. Add more or less to your liking and remember to pick a variety of colors of grape tomatoes if you can find them locally. Making colorful meals will get your baby used to seeing a rainbow of wonderful things to eat.

Yields 6 servings

1 cup water
3 cups cauliflower florets
2 tablespoons plant-based butter
½ cup grape tomatoes
1 teaspoon nutritional yeast
1 teaspoon Italian seasoning

1. In a medium saucepan over medium-high heat, add water and bring to a boil. Add cauliflower to a steamer insert and set into saucepan. Cover and steam about 12 minutes until tender.

2. Meanwhile, in a medium skillet over medium heat, warm the butter. Add tomatoes, nutritional yeast, and Italian seasoning; sauté about 3 minutes until heated through. Remove from heat.

3. Using a slotted spoon, transfer cauliflower to a food processor (reserve the cooking liquid for thinning). Add tomatoes. Pulse to a semi-smooth consistency. Add a little of the reserved water to thin if necessary to achieve desired consistency. Serve warm.

WHAT IS NUTRITIONAL YEAST?

Nutritional yeast is a food additive that has a cheesy and nutty flavor and dissolves when it cooks so you don't even realize it is there. It doesn't contain active yeast cells because they are killed during the manufacturing process. Nutritional yeast is a great source of protein and B vitamins. You can omit nutritional yeast from any of the recipes in this book if you choose. Bob's Red Mill is a popular and easy-to-find brand.

LOADED VEGETABLE MASHED POTATOES

When eating a plant-based diet, starchy foods are essential for getting enough calories. The potatoes carry the bulk of the calories here and are very satisfying. Serve this with a side dish of puréed beans, or feel free to add beans to this purée for protein.

Yields 8 servings

2 cups water

4 medium baking potatoes, **peeled and chopped**

¼ **cup diced** red bell pepper

½ **cup chopped zucchini**

¼ **cup diced yellow onion**

½ **cup chopped broccoli**

2 teaspoons plant-based butter, plus more for serving

½ **teaspoon garlic powder**

1 teaspoon chopped fresh parsley

1. In a medium saucepan over medium-high heat, combine water and potatoes. Bring to a boil. Reduce heat to medium and simmer about 10 minutes until tender, stirring occasionally.

2. Using a slotted spoon, transfer potatoes to a medium bowl and mash with a potato masher or fork. Add some of the cooking water and mash until the potatoes are a semi-smooth consistency. Set aside.

3. In a small skillet over medium heat, combine pepper, zucchini, onion, broccoli, 2 teaspoons butter, garlic powder, and parsley. Sauté about 5 minutes until onion is translucent and fragrant.

4. Combine sautéed ingredients with mashed potatoes. Serve warm with remaining butter.

CINNAMON-APPLESAUCE YOGURT

Save time by purchasing plain organic applesauce from the store. Adding the cinnamon makes the prepared applesauce taste more like homemade.

Yields 2 servings

½ cup plain oat milk yogurt alternative
¼ cup applesauce
Pinch ground cinnamon

1. In a small bowl, add yogurt and stir well to mix the creamy top layer with the rest of the yogurt.

2. Stir applesauce into yogurt.

3. Add cinnamon and mix thoroughly. Serve immediately.

SWEET PEAS WITH ORZO
(PICTURED)

Orzo pasta adds a good texture to this purée. Alternatively, you can substitute arborio rice if you wish.

Yields 1 serving

2 tablespoons cooked orzo pasta
¼ cup Sweet Pea Purée
(see recipe in Chapter 4)

1. In a small bowl, combine all ingredients.

2. If necessary, use a food processor to blend until a semi-smooth consistency is reached. Serve immediately.

KNOW YOUR PASTA

Although many mistake it for rice, orzo is actually pasta made from hard-wheat semolina. It makes a great substitute for arborio rice used in risotto and other recipes.

CINNAMON PEAS GALORE

Peas are a food that most babies enjoy. Try serving this recipe as a side dish at your family dinner. Even though it seems unusual, you'll be surprised! Instead of puréeing, serve the peas whole and top with plant-based butter and cinnamon. You can freeze remaining portions of this dish for later use.

Yields 8 servings

1 cup water
1 cup frozen peas
½ teaspoon ground cinnamon
Pat unsalted plant-based butter

1. In a medium saucepan over medium-high heat, add water and bring to a boil. Add peas to a steamer insert and set into saucepan. Cover and steam 5–7 minutes until tender.

2. Using a slotted spoon, transfer peas to a blender and add cinnamon. Purée until smooth and place in serving bowl. Stir in butter until it dissolves. Serve warm.

GARLIC MASHED POTATOES

Fresh garlic adds a great flavor to potatoes. Make a big pot of this dish for everyone in the family to enjoy. Serve with a side of beans and a vegetable purée for a complete dinner.

Yields 8–12 servings

2 cups water
4 medium baking potatoes, peeled and chopped
1 clove garlic, peeled and pressed
1 tablespoon plant-based butter

1. In a medium saucepan over medium-high heat, add water and potatoes. Bring to a boil.

2. Reduce heat to medium and add garlic. Simmer about 10 minutes until tender, stirring occasionally.

3. Using a slotted spoon, transfer potatoes to a medium bowl and mash with a potato masher or fork. Add some cooking water and mash until the potatoes are a semi-smooth consistency, or purée in a blender to achieve desired consistency.

4. Add butter and stir to combine. Serve warm. Freeze any remaining portions.

TWO-POTATO DREAM

The two flavors of sweet and buttery collide in this wonderful duo. If you'd like, instead of blending together, cook and blend the potatoes separately and then swirl the two purées together with a butter knife for an interesting effect. If your baby can tolerate it, skip the peeling and leave on the rinsed peel of the potato. The peel is very nutritious and has fiber that your baby needs.

Yields 6 servings

1 small Yukon Gold potato, **peeled and quartered**

1 small sweet potato, peeled and cut into 2" chunks

1 teaspoon plant-based butter, plus more for serving

½ cup water

1. In a small saucepan, add potatoes, butter, and water. Bring to a boil and cook until potatoes fall apart when pierced with a fork, about 15 minutes.

2. Transfer potatoes to a food processor. Process until smooth.

3. Place in a small bowl and stir in additional butter if desired. Serve warm.

GINGERED PEAR CRISP

The ginger in this recipe adds a little kick to the pear. It's just enough to add flavor, but take care not to overdo it and over-spice this dish.

Yields 4 servings

⅛ teaspoon ground ginger

1 medium ripe pear, **peeled, cored, and chopped**

Plain instant oats

1. In a medium nonstick saucepan over medium-low heat, combine ginger and pear.

2. Cover and cook about 7 minutes until pears are tender. Stir frequently.

3. Transfer pears to a food processor and purée to a semi-smooth consistency.

4. Fold in oats and serve immediately.

GARDEN VEGETABLE AND LENTIL DINNER

Lentils feature prominently in cuisines around the world, including the Middle East and India. Serve them to adults as a soup by adding spices and more broth if desired. For your baby, try this delicious dish. You can freeze remaining portions up to 8 weeks.

Yields 4–6 servings

1 tablespoon extra-virgin olive oil
2 tablespoons chopped carrot
2 tablespoons chopped celery
2 tablespoons chopped Vidalia onion
2 cups vegetable stock
½ cup dried brown lentils, picked over and rinsed
2 tablespoons chopped tomatoes

1. In a medium saucepan over medium heat, heat oil. Add carrot, celery, and onion, and sauté about 5 minutes until onion is translucent.

2. Add stock, lentils, and tomatoes, and bring to a boil over medium-high heat.

3. Reduce heat to low and simmer gently partly covered 30–45 minutes until lentils are tender.

4. Transfer to a blender and purée to desired consistency. Serve immediately.

LOVE LENTILS

Lentils are rich in iron and promote healthy brain development. These heart-healthy legumes are sold in green, red, or brown colors, whole or split. Store dried lentils in an airtight container in your pantry up to 12 months.

SOYBEAN PURÉE

If your child cannot digest soy-based formula, consult with your pediatrician prior to making this recipe to ensure no allergies to soy exist.

Yields 6 servings

½ cup dry soybeans, picked over and rinsed
2 cups water

1. In a small saucepan, combine soybeans with enough water to cover. Soak overnight in the refrigerator.

2. In the morning, drain the pot. Add water and set over medium-high heat. Bring to a boil, then reduce heat to low and simmer 2–2½ hours until soybeans are tender.

3. Drain and transfer soybeans to a food processor. Purée, while gradually adding water as needed to reach a smooth consistency. Serve immediately.

TOFU AND STRAWBERRY PURÉE

Because tofu is considered a soy product (and therefore on the allergenic list), make sure your pediatrician gives a thumbs-up before making this recipe. Tofu is a great source of protein for those who prefer plant-based protein instead of meat.

Yields 2 servings

1 cup whole strawberries, hulled and chopped
¼ cup chopped silken tofu

Add all ingredients to a food processor and process until smooth. Serve immediately.

CLEAN THOSE BERRIES

Make sure your strawberries are squeaky clean by soaking them 5 minutes in salt and vinegar. Cover them with water, add 2 teaspoons salt and 2 tablespoons distilled white vinegar. Gently rub them with your hands, and watch all the dirt fall to the bottom like magic. Rinse three times and then cut off the stems. All clean!

MINTED PEAS

Don't know what to do with all the mint growing in your yard? Use some of it to make this minty recipe for your baby. If your baby isn't sweet on the mint, you can use fresh chopped parsley or dill for a different flavor.

Yields 8 servings

1 cup water
2 cups frozen sweet peas
½ teaspoon fresh chopped mint
Pat plant-based butter, for serving

1. In a medium saucepan over medium-high heat, add water and bring to a boil. Add peas to a steamer insert and set into saucepan. Cover and steam about 10 minutes until tender. Cool slightly.

2. Using a slotted spoon, transfer peas to a food processor (reserve the cooking liquid for thinning). Add mint.

3. Pulse a few times and add a little reserved water if needed to reach a semi-smooth consistency.

4. Add butter before serving. Serve warm.

MELON-YOGURT CHILL-OUT

Chill out by the pool and enjoy this refreshing treat with your baby. Feel the breeze as you mash up this purée on the spot without a blender—no equipment necessary! Make sure the melon is ripe enough for mashing.

Yields 3 servings

1 slice honeydew melon, peeled and seeded
6 ounces oat milk yogurt alternative

1. Place melon on a plate and mash with a fork.

2. Stir in yogurt and mix thoroughly. Serve immediately.

MELON SUBSTITUTIONS

Watermelon or cantaloupe will also work well in this recipe. Simply substitute them for the honeydew melon and follow the instructions as written.

PURÉED BROWN RICE

Hooray! After 2 months of simple rice cereal, it's time for rice with more texture. Your baby will enjoy mashing this with his gums. Feel free to serve this any time of day.

Yields 2 servings

¼ cup uncooked brown rice
½ cup vegetable stock, plus more for thinning

1. In a small saucepan over medium-high heat, combine rice and stock. Bring to a boil.

2. Cover, reduce heat to low, and simmer 35 minutes until stock is completely absorbed.

3. Allow rice to cool; then transfer to food processor or blender. Pulse 30 seconds.

4. Add more stock to thin if necessary to achieve desired consistency. Serve immediately.

PEACH QUEEN

Quinoa, also known as the "mother of all grains," adds nice texture and a serving of whole grains to the smoothness of the Peach Purée. Quinoa offers iron, fiber, magnesium, and phosphorous, all essential for your baby's healthy development.

Yields 1 serving

¼ cup Peach Purée **(see recipe in Chapter 4)**

1 tablespoon cooked Basic Quinoa **(see recipe in this chapter)**

In a small bowl, combine Peach Purée and Basic Quinoa. Serve immediately.

SECURE THE FEEDING BOWL

Around 10 months old, babies enjoy learning how to feed themselves. Sometimes this can become a messy feat, especially when her curiosity over the bowl piques and she picks it up and tosses it across the room! Avoid this by purchasing feeding dishes that have suction cups at the bottom that can attach to high-chair trays.

PEAR OATMEAL

Ever heard of Pear Oatmeal? That's the beauty of making your own purées. You can make flavor combinations that you won't find at the store.

Yields 2 servings

¼ cup old-fashioned oats (not quick-cooking)

1 cup water

½ very ripe medium pear, peeled, cored, and diced

1. Using either a food processor or blender, grind oats into a fine powder. A mortar and pestle also makes a terrific grinder for a small amount.

2. In a small saucepan, bring water to a boil. Add oats, stirring constantly 30 seconds.

3. Cover the pot, reduce heat to low, and simmer 8–10 minutes until oats are smooth and thick. Stir occasionally to prevent sticking and burning.

4. Transfer pear to a plate and fork-mash until completely smooth.

5. Place oats in a small bowl and mix in pear. Serve immediately.

DON'T SKIP OUT ON SNACKS

Even a hearty meal such as oatmeal or a stew won't be enough to tide your baby over until lunch. Babies need to eat every couple of hours no matter what. Actually, eating small portions every 2 or 3 hours is healthier for everyone for sustained energy and body metabolism.

POPEYE'S SPINACH MEAL

If the flavor of spinach seems too strong for baby, mixing it with potato will make it more acceptable.

Yields 6 servings

½ small yellow onion, peeled and chopped
1 medium baking potato, peeled and chopped
½ cup water
1 cup chopped fresh baby spinach
Pat plant-based butter, for serving

1. In a deep medium nonstick skillet over medium-high heat, add onion and sauté until soft and translucent, about 3 minutes.

2. Add potato and water. Bring to a boil, then reduce heat and simmer 15–20 minutes until potato is tender. Add spinach.

3. In a food processor, add potato mixture. Purée until smooth, adding as much water as necessary for age-appropriate consistency. Remove and transfer to a serving bowl.

4. Add butter before serving. Serve warm.

GIVE YOUR GREENS A BATH

Get rid of all the dirt and sand found in fresh leafy greens like spinach, collards, and kale by making a bath for them in your kitchen sink. Submerge the greens in a large bowl of water and allow them to soak for a few minutes. Drain. Repeat the process until the water is clear.

PUMPKIN "CREAM" PIE
(PICTURED)

Pumpkin pie isn't just for big kids and older adults. Babies can have it too! This recipe combines the autumn richness of pumpkin with a creamy yet crunchy bite.

Yields 2 servings

½ cup canned pure pumpkin or Pumpkin Purée (see recipe in Chapter 4)

2 tablespoons almond flour

1 tablespoon coconut milk yogurt alternative

⅛ teaspoon ground cinnamon

In a medium bowl, combine all ingredients and serve immediately.

BASIC QUINOA

This healthy grain boasts fiber, essential amino acids, and protein. Thoroughly rinse quinoa under running water before cooking.

Yields 8 servings

1 cup quinoa

2 cups water

1. In a medium saucepan over medium-high heat, combine quinoa and water. Bring to a boil.

2. Reduce heat, cover, and simmer 15 minutes until the outer ring of each grain separates.

3. Fluff before serving. Serve warm.

RASPBERRY-PEAR PURÉE

The hue of raspberries adds a splash of color to this dish, which your baby can enjoy any time of the year.

Yields 4 servings

1 medium apple, peeled, cored, and sliced
½ medium pear, peeled, cored, and sliced
¼ cup raspberries

1. In a medium saucepan over medium-high heat, combine apple and pear slices.

2. Add raspberries. Add enough water to cover and bring to a boil. Reduce heat to medium-low and simmer about 25 minutes until apple and pear are completely tender.

3. Using a slotted spoon, transfer fruit into a food processor. Process until mixture is semi-smooth, adding water if needed to thin.

4. Pour purée through a fine-mesh strainer to remove any seeds if desired. Serve immediately.

RUTABAGA AND PEAR MEDLEY

Rutabagas are beta-carotene-rich root vegetables that grow best in cold climates, such as the northern United States and Canada.

Yields 4 servings

1 medium rutabaga, trimmed, peeled, and coarsely chopped
¼ cup water
1 small ripe pear, peeled, cored, and chopped

1. In a small saucepan over medium-high heat, combine rutabaga and water. Bring to a boil. Boil about 10 minutes until soft.

2. Transfer rutabaga, pear, and reserved water to a blender. Purée until mixture is semi-smooth. Add more water if necessary to thin. Serve chilled.

SUMMERTIME PEACH-RASPBERRY DELIGHT

This charming dessert purée offers a dose of vitamin C and lycopene, which protects cells from damage.

Yields 6-8 servings

1 cup raspberries
5 small peaches, peeled, pitted, and chopped

1. Wash raspberries and drain, but do not dry.

2. Transfer moist raspberries and chopped peaches to a blender and purée until smooth.

3. Press purée through a fine-mesh strainer to remove raspberry seeds.

4. Serve chilled.

PURÉED COLLARD GREENS

Although collards and other leafy greens contain nitrates, by 8 months old your baby can safely have these leafy greens. Spinach and kale are great substitutes for the collards in this recipe. You can also add texture to this purée by adding crumbles of soft cornbread.

Yields 4 servings

4 cups trimmed collard greens
2 cups vegetable stock or water
2 tablespoons chopped yellow onion
1 clove garlic, peeled and pressed
1 tablespoon extra-virgin olive oil

1. In a medium saucepan over medium-high heat, combine collards, stock, onion, and garlic.

2. Boil about 15 minutes until vegetables turn a bright-green color. Allow greens to cool.

3. Using a slotted spoon, transfer greens to blender. Add oil.

4. Purée while gradually adding cooking liquid until smooth. Serve immediately.

CINNAMON-DATE MASH
(PICTURED)

Dates are very sweet and can be used as a natural, plant-based sweetener or served alone. Dates are high in fiber and help with digestion, boost the immune system, promote healthy eyesight, and more!

Yields 10 servings

1 cup medium pitted dates
1 cup boiling water
½ teaspoon ground cinnamon

1. Add dates to a medium glass bowl. Add boiling water and allow to soak 3–4 hours until dates are completely hydrated and soft.

2. Remove softened dates, reserving soaking water, and transfer to a food processor. Add cinnamon. Add reserved soaking water a little at a time to achieve desired consistency. Process until semi-smooth. Serve immediately.

SAUTÉED BROCCOLI PURÉE

Broccoli is high in fiber and vitamin C, so serve up this meal as a side dish to your baby's main course a few times per week. Double this recipe and combine all ingredients in a skillet and cook until broccoli is tender for the rest of the family to enjoy.

Yields 4 servings

1 cup water
2 cups broccoli florets
1 tablespoon extra-virgin olive oil
½ tablespoon plant-based butter

1. In a medium saucepan over medium-high heat, add water and bring to a boil. Add broccoli to a steamer insert and set into saucepan. Cover and steam about 10 minutes until tender.

2. In a medium skillet over medium-high heat, add oil and tilt to coat skillet. Add broccoli and butter and sauté 5 minutes. Remove from heat.

3. Transfer sautéed broccoli to blender. Process until semi-smooth. Add more water if necessary to thin. Serve warm.

SQUASH AND CORN COMBO

This recipe serves up the yellow in the rainbow of foods. Be sure to make this purée smooth; there should be no indigestible fibers from the corn.

Yields 6 servings

½ cup chopped butternut squash
½ cup water
¼ cup frozen corn kernels

1. In a medium saucepan over medium-high heat, combine squash, water, and corn. Bring to a boil.

2. Stir frequently while cooking to ensure that squash cooks evenly. Cook 8–10 minutes until tender.

3. Using a slotted spoon, transfer to a food processor or blender. Purée while gradually adding just enough water to achieve a smooth consistency. Serve warm.

SUPERSTAR SPINACH ROTINI

If baby takes an interest in self-feeding, allow her to experiment eating this dish with her hands. Just make sure you cover the floor!

Yields 3 servings

¼ cup chopped uncooked rotini pasta
1 cup chopped baby spinach
2 tablespoons water

1. In a medium saucepan over medium-high heat, combine pasta with enough water to cover. Boil 8 minutes until pasta is very tender.

2. In a medium saucepan over medium heat, sauté spinach with 2 tablespoons water 2 minutes until wilted.

3. Using a slotted spoon, transfer cooked spinach to a food processor. Process until semi-smooth.

4. Fold in chopped pasta. Serve warm.

SWEET POTATO AND PEACH PERFECTION

The brilliant colors of orange in this recipe indicate an abundant presence of vitamin C and beta-carotene.

Yields 3 servings

½ small sweet potato
1 medium ripe peach, peeled and diced

1. Preheat oven to 375°F.

2. Poke several holes in sweet potato. Bake 40 minutes. Let stand until cool enough to handle.

3. Scoop potato out of the peel and into a bowl. Toss in diced peaches. Serve chilled.

TURNIP AND SWEET POTATO MASH

Turnips come in purple, white, and green. It doesn't matter which one you choose; they are all white on the inside!

Yields 1 serving

1 small turnip, peeled and chopped
¼ cup water
¼ cup Sweet Potato Purée
(see recipe in Chapter 4)

1. In a small saucepan over medium-high heat, combine turnip and water.

2. Bring to a boil. Reduce heat to medium and simmer 20 minutes until turnip is tender.

3. Using a slotted spoon, transfer turnip to a food processor. Process until semi-smooth.

4. In a small bowl, combine turnip purée with Sweet Potato Purée. Serve warm.

BASIL 'N' BLUEBERRIES

This is an unexpected flavor pairing and gives the blueberries a unique yet yummy taste! Feel free to serve as-is or use as a topping with any oatmeal or plant-based ice cream.

Yields 2 servings

½ cup blueberries
1 tablespoon chopped fresh basil
¼ cup water

1. In a small saucepan over medium heat, combine all ingredients.

2. Cook until blueberries start to burst open, about 5 minutes.

3. Transfer to a blender and pulse until semi-smooth. Serve immediately.

APPLE AND CUCUMBER PURÉE

Babies need healthy fat at this stage for proper brain development. Adding 1 teaspoon of coconut oil or plant-based butter to your baby's meals will ensure he is getting enough food and feeling satisfied. The rosemary adds a savory touch to this purée.

Yields 6 servings

2 large apples, peeled, cored, and quartered
¼ teaspoon dried rosemary
1 tablespoon water
½ medium cucumber, peeled (optional) and cut into large pieces
1 teaspoon coconut oil (optional)

1. In a small saucepan over medium heat, add apples, rosemary, and water. Cook 10 minutes until tender, stirring occasionally. Cool completely.

2. Combine cucumber, coconut oil (if desired), and cooked apple mixture in a food processor. Process until semi-smooth. Serve immediately.

APPLE AND SQUASH TOSS-UP

Apples and squash are a traditional pairing in family meals, especially during the winter holidays. This recipe brings the flavor of the holidays into a purée, featuring cinnamon and cardamom spices for a delightful blend.

Yields 2 servings

½ cup chopped butternut squash
½ cup peeled and chopped Gala apples
⅛ teaspoon ground cinnamon
⅛ teaspoon ground cardamom
¼ cup water

1. In a medium saucepan over medium heat, add all ingredients. Cover and cook 10–15 minutes until squash and apples are fork-tender. Remove from heat and cool slightly.

2. Using a slotted spoon, transfer mixture to a food processor and pulse to combine. Continue to process until a semi-smooth consistency is reached. Serve warm.

AVOCADO AND BEET PURÉE

The velvety texture of beets makes a great complement to that of avocados. Beets are known to boost the immune system, and because they are rich in antioxidants, they may help to reduce the risk of cancer. Beets are rich in folate and contain vitamin C, potassium, iron, magnesium, and copper. Purchasing cooked beets is a great way to save time in making this purée.

Yields 2 servings

½ medium ripe avocado, pitted and peeled
1 small beet, peeled and cooked
1 teaspoon fresh lime juice

Add all ingredients to a food processor and purée until smooth. Serve immediately.

AVOCADO AND PAPAYA PURÉE

This dish is a great combination that's rich in healthy monounsaturated fat, vitamin C, vitamin A, and fiber. Ripe papaya adds a wonderful flavor when combined with the avocado.

Yields 4 servings

½ medium ripe avocado, pitted and peeled
1 teaspoon fresh lime juice
½ cup cubed papaya

1. Add avocado to a small bowl. Drizzle with lime juice.

2. Transfer avocado to a food processor. Add papaya and purée until smooth. Serve immediately.

AVOCADO AND STRAWBERRY DELIGHT

Because avocados are a nutrient-dense food filled with healthy goodness in a small package, serve them often so your baby can get used to the flavor and texture. This recipe adds the sweetness of strawberries with a hint of lime flavor, which in the adult word is strawberry guacamole!

Yields 2 servings

½ medium ripe avocado, pitted and peeled
1 teaspoon fresh lime juice
¼ cup puréed strawberries

1. Add avocado to a small bowl. Drizzle with lime juice and mash with a fork until smooth.

2. Add strawberry purée and mix well to combine. Serve immediately.

STRAWBERRY, CUCUMBER, AND BASIL PURÉE

Basil is super easy to grow indoors or out. You can start from seeds or buy a plant or two to have unlimited basil to add to your baby's meals. Herbs are a great way to add some new flavor to growing taste buds.

Yields 4 servings

1 teaspoon finely chopped fresh basil
1 cup whole strawberries**, hulled**
½ cup sliced English cucumber

Add all ingredients to a food processor and purée until a semi-smooth consistency is reached. Add water or your favorite milk to thin if needed. Serve chilled.

BEET AND BLUEBERRY PURÉE

Beets have a natural sweet flavor and are brimming with antioxidants. Combined with the blueberries, this dish is a powerful meal that protects against free radicals and improves heart health, reduces cancer risk, and supports mental health. Beets come in different varieties, including red, white, and golden. Choose whatever is available in your area. They all have the same amazing health benefits.

Yields 4 servings

1 large red or golden beet, trimmed, peeled, and cut into large pieces
½ cup blueberries

1. In a medium saucepan over medium-high heat, combine beets with enough water to cover. Bring to a boil.

2. Reduce heat to medium and cook 12–15 minutes until beets can be easily pierced with a fork.

3. Remove from the heat and allow to cool 5 minutes.

4. Transfer beets and blueberries to a food processor. Purée about 15 seconds until a smooth consistency is reached. Add more water if needed. Serve warm or chilled.

BRAZILIAN COCONUT RICE

You can add instant Brazilian flare to plain brown rice by adding coconut milk. While this recipe calls for Puréed Brown Rice, feel free to substitute the brown rice for fragrant brown jasmine rice for a more authentic taste.

Yields 2 servings

¼ cup Puréed Brown Rice (see recipe in this chapter)

1 tablespoon unsweetened canned coconut milk

½ teaspoon plant-based butter

In a small bowl, combine all ingredients. Serve warm.

BUTTERNUT SQUASH BISQUE

As your baby moves on from single-ingredient purées, it's time to step up the purée game and add more ingredients to ensure she's getting plenty of nutritional benefits. Adding onions and peppers is a great way to bring the flavor up a notch, but they offer plenty of benefits too!

Yields 10 servings

1 large butternut squash, halved lengthwise and seeded

3 tablespoons plant-based butter, divided

1 clove garlic, peeled and pressed

¼ cup chopped yellow onion

1 small red bell pepper, seeded and chopped

2 cups Vegetable Stock (see recipe in Chapter 4)

¼ teaspoon salt

⅛ teaspoon ground nutmeg

¼ cup canned coconut cream

1. Preheat oven to 375°F. Line a large baking sheet with foil.

2. Pierce the skin of the squash a few times with a fork. Place cut-side down on prepared baking sheet. Bake 40 minutes until the flesh is tender. Remove from heat and set aside.

3. In a large saucepan over medium heat, add 2 tablespoons butter, garlic, onion, and pepper. Sauté, stirring occasionally, about 5 minutes until onion is translucent.

4. Scoop flesh from squash into the saucepan along with Vegetable Stock and remaining 1 tablespoon butter. Bring to a boil. Reduce heat to low and simmer 15 minutes.

5. Transfer soup to a blender and purée until smooth. Return bisque to saucepan over low heat and add salt and nutmeg. Cook until heated through. Garnish each serving with a dollop of coconut cream. Serve immediately.

CHERRIES AND SQUASH PURÉE

Cherries and squash make a fantastic flavor combination that's also full of plenty of immunity-boosting nutrients.

Yields 4 servings

1 cup water
½ cup pitted cherries
½ cup cubed butternut squash

1. In a medium saucepan over medium-high heat, add water and bring to a boil. Add cherries and squash to a steamer insert and set into saucepan. Cover and steam about 10 minutes until tender.

2. Using a slotted spoon, transfer squash and cherries to a food processor (reserve the cooking liquid for thinning). Process until smooth. Add a little of the reserved water if needed to achieve desired consistency. Serve warm.

PEAR AND BLUEBERRY PURÉE

If you're looking for a quick purée that explodes with taste and nutrition, look no further! This purée adds a serving of greens, although no one would know. The mint adds value too! Mint aids in digestion and keeps harmful bacteria at bay—although keep in mind that not all children tolerate mint well. Serve this meal for an instant immunity boost.

Yields 4 servings

2 medium Bartlett pears**, peeled, cored, and chopped**
½ cup blueberries
⅓ cup baby spinach
1 tablespoon chopped fresh mint

1. In a medium saucepan over medium heat, combine all ingredients. Cover and cook 5 minutes.

2. Using a slotted spoon, transfer ingredients to a food processor. Purée until a semi-smooth consistency is reached. Serve immediately.

PEAR, SPINACH, AND PEA PURÉE
(PICTURED)

This is a super healthy purée that adds the sweet flavor of pear to ignite the senses. This is yummy served with quinoa or oatmeal cereal.

Yields 2 servings

½ cup chopped pear

¼ cup frozen peas, steamed

½ cup baby spinach

Add all ingredients to a food processor. Pulse until a semi-smooth consistency is reached. Serve immediately.

CARROT, PARSNIP, AND POTATO MASH

Herbs unite with root vegetables in this garlicky purée. Serve with a side of leafy green purée such as collards or spinach.

Yields 4 servings

2 medium parsnips, peeled and cut into large pieces

2 medium carrots, peeled and cut into large pieces

1 large russet potato, peeled and cut into large pieces

1 teaspoon minced garlic

1 teaspoon chopped fresh parsley

2 teaspoons plant-based butter

⅓ cup vegetable stock or water

1. In a medium saucepan over medium heat, add all ingredients.

2. Cook 15–20 minutes until vegetables are fork-tender.

3. Transfer to a medium bowl and mash with a fork, or cut into bite-sized pieces for your baby to self-feed. Serve warm.

PEAS AND CARROTS PURÉE

Peas are full of protein and are an excellent source of vitamin C and fiber. Combining these cuties with carrots adds beta-carotene, which the body converts to vitamin A to help maintain healthy eyes, teeth, skin, and bones.

Yields 2 servings

1 cup water
½ cup frozen sweet peas
½ cup chopped carrots

1. In a medium saucepan over medium-high heat, add water and bring to a boil. Add peas and carrots to a steamer insert and set into saucepan. Cover and steam about 3–5 minutes until tender.

2. Using a slotted spoon, transfer peas and carrots to a food processor. Pulse to combine until semi-smooth. Add water or your favorite thinning liquid as necessary to achieve desired consistency. Serve warm.

PEAS AND LEEKS PURÉE

This purée is so versatile it can be combined with other vegetables such as mashed Yukon Gold potatoes, red-skinned potatoes, or sweet potatoes. If frozen, it can also be added to many of the recipes in this book, such as Lemony Zoodles or Chickpea Rotini Pasta with Mushroom Sauce (see recipes in Chapter 7).

Yields 4 servings

1 cup frozen sweet peas
⅓ cup thinly sliced leeks
½ cup Vegetable Stock (see recipe in Chapter 4)

1. In a medium saucepan over medium heat, add all ingredients. Bring to a boil.

2. Reduce heat to low, cover, and simmer 5 minutes. Remove from heat and cool 3–5 minutes.

3. Using a slotted spoon, transfer peas and leeks to a food processor, reserving remaining stock in the saucepan. Pulse until semi-smooth. Continue to process while adding a little of the stock at a time to reach a semi-smooth consistency. Serve warm.

RASPBERRY-ZUCCHINI PURÉE

Raspberries and zucchini unite in this simple yet fruity purée. Zucchini are in abundance during the summer, so use them up and give this purée a try. Its flavor is sure to please, and the raspberries deliver some amazing health benefits, as they are rich in antioxidants.

Yields 4 servings

1 cup water
1 cup chopped zucchini
½ cup raspberries

1. In a medium saucepan over medium-high heat, add water and bring to a boil. Add zucchini to a steamer insert and set into saucepan. Cover and steam 3 minutes.

2. Using a slotted spoon, transfer zucchini to a food processor. Add raspberries and purée until a semi-smooth consistency is reached. Serve immediately.

SOUTHERN LIMA BEAN PURÉE

Baby lima beans are smaller and creamier than traditional lima beans. However, you can use regular lima beans if you have them on hand. Like other beans, baby limas pack a lot of fiber and plant-powered protein.

Yields 4 servings

1 cup frozen baby lima beans
2 cups Vegetable Stock (see recipe in Chapter 4)
1 teaspoon plant-based butter
1 tablespoon diced yellow onion
⅛ teaspoon smoked paprika (optional)

1. In a medium saucepan over low heat, combine all ingredients. Cover and simmer 20–25 minutes until beans are very tender.

2. Using a slotted spoon, transfer vegetables to a food processor. Process until the mixture is a semi-smooth purée. Add more stock if necessary to thin. Serve warm.

SPINACH, AVOCADO, AND BANANA PURÉE
(PICTURED)

Dark-green leafy vegetables offer a full spectrum of nutrients that no animal product can touch! The sweet banana in this purée offsets some of the bitterness of the spinach. Add more or less if you desire.

Yields 4 servings

½ medium banana, peeled and sliced
1 tablespoon avocado pulp
1 teaspoon fresh lime juice
¼ cup puréed baby spinach

1. In a medium bowl, add banana and avocado. Drizzle with lime juice. Mash banana and avocado until smooth with a fork.

2. Add spinach and stir to combine. Serve immediately.

CHERRY PURÉE

Cherries are a delightful fruit brimming with antioxidants. Choose beautiful, deep-red cherries that are free of blemishes and pesticides for best results. Cherries pair extremely well with other purées such as pear, peach, plum, banana, and apple. Have fun playing with any of those combinations.

Yields 8 servings

12 whole cherries, pitted

Place cherries in a food processor and process until semi-smooth. Add water as needed to thin. Serve immediately.

SPINACH AND MANGO PURÉE

This purée combines the tropical flavor of mango with the nutritional boost of dark leafy greens.

Yields 2 servings

¼ **cup puréed** spinach

½ **cup Mango Purée (see recipe in Chapter 4)**

1 **tablespoon unsweetened canned coconut milk**

In a medium bowl, combine all ingredients. Serve immediately.

ROASTED BUTTERNUT SQUASH AND CRANBERRY PURÉE

Although there are many options to cook squash and cranberries, this recipe combines them in a lovely way and gives you time to get other things done while it's cooking. For adults, cooking the cranberries in the cavity of the squash and drizzling it with maple syrup adds an instant gourmet presentation to your holiday dinner table.

Yields 10 servings

1 **large butternut squash, halved lengthwise and seeded**

⅓ **cup fresh cranberries**

⅓ **cup chopped dates**

1. Preheat oven to 375°F. Line a large baking sheet with foil.

2. Pierce the outside of the squash a few times with a fork. Place cut-side up on the baking sheet. Spoon cranberries and dates into squash cavity.

3. Bake 40 minutes until squash is tender and cranberries have burst. Remove from heat and set aside.

4. Scoop the flesh, berries, and dates from squash skin and add to a food processor. Process until semi-smooth. Add water as necessary to achieve desired consistency. Serve warm.

SPICED SQUASH AND PEAR PURÉE

Adding mild spices such as ginger and nutmeg really wakes up the flavor of pears and squash. If you don't have those spices, feel free to substitute ground cinnamon, allspice, or ground cloves.

½ cup chopped butternut squash
½ cup chopped Bartlett pears
⅛ teaspoon ground ginger
⅛ teaspoon ground nutmeg
¼ cup water

1. In a medium saucepan over medium heat, add all ingredients. Cover and cook 10–15 minutes until squash and pears are fork-tender. Remove from heat and cool slightly.

2. Using a slotted spoon, transfer all ingredients to a food processor and pulse to combine. Continue to process until a semi-smooth consistency is reached. Serve warm.

SWEET POTATO AND CAULIFLOWER PURÉE

This simple yet flavorful purée doesn't take a lot of preparation and is rich and satisfying. The starch from the potatoes adds that stick-to-your-ribs goodness.

1 cup water
1 medium sweet potato, peeled and cut into large pieces
½ cup cauliflower florets
Oat milk, for thinning
2 teaspoons plant-based butter
⅛ teaspoon ground nutmeg

1. In a medium saucepan over medium-high heat, add water and bring to a boil. Add sweet potato and cauliflower to a steamer insert and set into saucepan. Cover and steam about 12–15 minutes until fork-tender.

2. Using a slotted spoon, transfer sweet potato and cauliflower to a food processor. Pulse a few times to combine. Add milk as needed to blend into a semi-smooth consistency.

3. Transfer purée into a medium bowl. Add butter and nutmeg, then stir to combine. Serve immediately.

SWEET POTATO AND PEAR MASH

Sweet potatoes are commonly prepared with apples and cranberries, but have you tried them with pears? This is a delicious twist on a classic tradition. Store extra portions of this dish in an airtight container in the refrigerator up to 4 days or freeze up to 8 weeks.

Yields 6 servings

2 large sweet potatoes, peeled and cut into 2" chunks

⅓ cup water

1 tablespoon coconut oil

½ teaspoon ground cardamom

1 medium pear, peeled, cored, and chopped

1. In a medium saucepan over medium-low heat, combine all ingredients. Cover and cook 15–20 minutes until sweet potatoes fall apart when pierced with a fork. Stir frequently. Remove from heat and cool slightly.

2. Mash all ingredients with a fork until semi-smooth. Serve immediately.

BANANA RICE CEREAL

Babies need complex carbohydrates to maintain a healthy weight. The bananas in this dish combined with the whole-grain rice provide sustained energy and fullness.

Yields 1 serving

¼ cup cooked brown rice, warmed

2 tablespoons mashed banana

½ teaspoon plant-based butter

2 tablespoons oat milk

In a small bowl, combine all ingredients. Serve warm.

HERBED CREAMED CORN

This is a flavorful herbed corn recipe that uses oat milk for creaminess. You'll never know it's there! Alternatively, soy milk or even vegan cream cheese can be used.

Yields 2 servings

1 teaspoon avocado oil
1 tablespoon minced yellow onion
1 clove garlic, peeled and minced
1 cup frozen corn kernels
1 teaspoon dried parsley
⅓ cup oat milk, plus more for thinning

1. In a medium skillet over medium heat, add oil, onion, and garlic. Sauté, stirring, 5 minutes until onion is translucent and garlic is fragrant.

2. Add remaining ingredients. Cook about 10 minutes until heated through.

3. Transfer all ingredients to a food processor and pulse a few times to break up the corn into smaller pieces. Add more milk to thin if necessary. Serve warm.

6

PLEASING AN EXPANDED PALATE:
CHUNKY PURÉES FOR LITTLE ONES
(10–12 MONTHS)

By now your baby should have a monster appetite, eating three meals and two snacks per day! She should be able to tolerate a chunky texture and can begin to self-feed, an important developmental step. This chapter introduces pasta and custards, foods that your baby is sure to enjoy and benefit from. The recipes in this chapter should be a chunky consistency, which can be achieved using the pulse setting on a blender or by mashing the food with a fork. Encourage exploration and allow your baby to feed herself purées with her hands or with an infant fork or spoon. Keep plenty of bibs on hand!

You can also introduce the sippy cup, and allow him to drink more fluids. He should still continue to drink 24–32 ounces of breast milk or iron-fortified infant plant-based formula per day. Expand the variety of cereals, fruits, vegetables, soft breads made from whole ingredients, and finger foods. Babies will take 1- to 2-ounce servings of each of these per day at this age.

Don't forget to use your previously frozen purées and combine them with pasta shapes, diced cooked vegetables, and plant-based yogurt, or use them as spreads for teething biscuits. Frozen purées can always be used, so don't let them go to waste!

PEAR-APRICOT MASH

This purée is loaded with vitamin C, iron, potassium, and beta-carotene. Use dried apricots instead of fresh if you like.

Yields 3 servings

1 cup water

1 medium pear, peeled, cored, and cut into large pieces

2 medium ripe apricots, pitted and halved

1. In a medium saucepan over medium-high heat, add water and bring to a boil. Add pear and apricots to a steamer insert and set into saucepan. Cover and steam 10 minutes until apricots are very soft.

2. Using a slotted spoon, transfer fruit to a plate. Remove skins from apricots by scooping the fruit out with a spoon. Mash fruit with a fork. Serve immediately.

WILD BANANAS 'N' BUTTER

This recipe introduces almond butter, a nutritious and tasty treat with many health benefits. Almond butter contains protein and healthy fat that's essential for baby's growth and development.

Yields 2 servings

1 medium banana, peeled

¼ teaspoon ground cinnamon

1 tablespoon smooth almond butter

1. In a small bowl, combine banana with cinnamon and mash with a fork until creamy.

2. Fold in almond butter. Serve immediately.

ALLERGY ALERT!

Although almonds are safe for babies to consume, if you or anyone in your family has a history of almond allergies, be sure to get the thumbs-up from your pediatrician before serving almond butter.

STRAWBERRY AND CANTALOUPE JOY

Cantaloupe and strawberries make a joyful combination for teething babies. The soft texture of cantaloupe is soothing on a baby's gums. You can also soothe baby's gums by freezing this purée and making a sorbet. Make sure the cantaloupe is fully ripe for best results.

Yields 2 servings

2 medium strawberries**, hulled and quartered**
1 cup chopped cantaloupe

Combine all ingredients in a food processor. Pulse a few times for a chunky purée. Serve immediately.

MINTED BANANAS AND STRAWBERRIES
(PICTURED)

You can't go wrong with bananas and strawberries. Liven up the combination with a touch of fresh mint, which you can find in the produce aisle at the grocery store.

Yields 4 servings

1 large banana, peeled and cut into baby bite-sized pieces
½ teaspoon fresh lemon juice
1 pint strawberries**, hulled and diced**
5 large fresh mint leaves, finely chopped

1. Place banana in a medium bowl. Drizzle with lemon juice to keep it from turning brown.

2. Add remaining ingredients. Mash with a fork into a rough chunky texture or serve as finger food.

PINEAPPLE CABBAGE

If your baby isn't sure about this dish, try offering it at another time. It may take a while before a child accepts new tastes and textures, but it's certainly worth the effort! Using the grater disk on your food processor will allow you to zip through shredding the cabbage in no time flat!

Yields 8 servings

½ medium head green cabbage, cored and shredded
½ cup pineapple chunks
½ cup water
½ tablespoon plant-based butter

1. In a large saucepan over medium heat, combine cabbage, pineapple, and water. Cover and cook 20 minutes until tender.

2. Using a slotted spoon, transfer cabbage and pineapple to a food processor. Pulse until a chunky consistency is reached. Transfer to a medium bowl and toss with butter. Serve warm.

BABY MUESLI

The breakfast cereal muesli, which means "mixture" in German, was first created by a Swiss nutritionist as a health food. Feel free to substitute different fruits and grains.

Yields 2 servings

¼ cup old-fashioned oats (not quick-cooking)
1 cup oat milk
½ medium banana, peeled and chopped
1 medium pear, peeled, cored, and chopped
2 medium apricots, peeled, pitted, and chopped

1. In a medium saucepan over medium-high heat, combine oats and milk. Bring to a boil, then cook 30 seconds.

2. Add chopped fruit and stir thoroughly.

3. Reduce heat to low, cover, and simmer 8–10 minutes until oats are smooth and thick. Stir occasionally to prevent sticking and burning.

4. Serve as is or purée in a food processor for a creamier texture.

RICE PUDDING

This popular dish ensures that your baby gets both the carbohydrates and calcium he needs for energy and strong bones.

Yields 2 servings

½ cup uncooked brown rice
1 cup water
1 cup oat milk

1. In a small saucepan over medium-high heat, combine rice and water and bring to a boil. Reduce heat to medium-low, cover, and simmer about 20 minutes until water is absorbed.

2. Add milk to rice and mix well.

3. Cook over medium heat 10 minutes, stirring often. Mixture will thicken.

4. Allow mixture to cool and mash with fork to desired consistency. Serve warm.

BABY RATATOUILLE

This is a baby-friendly version of a classic French comfort food that boasts a healthy trio of eggplant, zucchini, and tomatoes in a fragrant ratatouille sauce.

Yields 4 servings

1 tablespoon extra-virgin olive oil
½ small yellow onion, peeled and diced
½ small eggplant, diced
1 small zucchini, diced
1 (14.5-ounce) can diced tomatoes
½ teaspoon dried oregano
½ teaspoon dried parsley
½ teaspoon dried basil

1. In a medium saucepan over medium heat, heat oil. Add onion and sauté 3 minutes or until onions begin to turn translucent.

2. Add eggplant, zucchini, and tomatoes. Bring to a boil.

3. Reduce heat to medium-low and cook 20 minutes. Stir in herbs and cook another 20 minutes. Allow to cool, then fork-mash to desired consistency. Serve warm.

TOMATO AND MUSHROOM PASTA

Tomatoes grow effortlessly in a container or garden, and there are hundreds of varieties to choose from. The chickpea pasta called for here adds sufficient protein and fiber to this meal, making it complete.

Yields 2 servings

2 cups water

½ cup uncooked chickpea pasta

1 teaspoon extra-virgin olive oil

¼ cup white button mushrooms

1 medium tomato, cored and diced

⅛ teaspoon dried basil

1. In a medium saucepan over medium-high heat, bring water to a boil. Add pasta and cook 10–15 minutes until pasta is very tender.

2. In a small skillet over medium-high heat, heat oil. Add mushrooms and sauté 6–7 minutes until tender.

3. Add tomato and basil. Sauté 15–18 minutes until very tender.

4. Drain pasta and toss with mushroom mixture.

5. Allow to cool, then fork-mash to desired consistency. Serve warm.

FRUTTI-TUTTI TOFU

Silken tofu makes puréeing easy. Firmer tofu may need additional liquid and may not be as smooth. Look for tofu made with non-GM soybeans.

Yields 1 serving

¼ cup sliced peaches

2 tablespoons blueberries

1 tablespoon chopped fresh mint

1 ounce silken tofu

Combine all ingredients in a food processor. Pulse to achieve a chunky consistency. Serve immediately.

FREEZING TOFU

Freeze leftover tofu in small containers or ice cube trays. Freezing and thawing it tends to give it better absorbency. Adults may frown at the soggier texture, but your baby will love it!

GARLIC ASPARAGUS WITH DILL

Here is a tasty asparagus recipe for your baby. The extra-virgin olive oil and garlic really boost the nutritional value of this vegetable and provide the fatty acids needed to promote healthy brain development.

Yields 2 servings

6 medium asparagus spears, trimmed
½ tablespoon extra-virgin olive oil
1 teaspoon dried dill
1 clove garlic, peeled and pressed

1. Preheat oven to 400°F.

2. Place asparagus in a small baking dish and drizzle with oil. Sprinkle with dill and garlic.

3. Bake 20 minutes until tender.

4. Cut spears into thirds and transfer to a food processor. Process while adding water as needed to achieve a chunky consistency. Serve immediately.

BABY'S PEACHY COBBLER

The shortbread cookie replaces the traditional sweet biscuit or piecrust topping found in traditional peach cobbler. If your diet doesn't include any animal products, choose vegan shortbread cookies.

Yields 2 servings

1 medium peach, peeled and sliced thin
½ teaspoon coconut oil
⅛ teaspoon ground cinnamon
1 shortbread cookie, crushed

1. Preheat oven to 350°F. Grease a small baking dish.

2. In prepared baking dish, toss peach slices with oil and cinnamon.

3. Bake 30 minutes until peaches are completely soft.

4. Transfer peaches to a small bowl, and fork-mash to desired consistency. Top with a sprinkle of shortbread cookie pieces. Serve warm.

TOFU-VEGETABLE STIR-FRY
(PICTURED)

While a little work is needed to prepare all the vegetables, this recipe makes enough to serve again throughout the week. It's a delicious and satisfying complete meal for everyone. If you can't find coconut aminos, use organic tamari soy sauce instead.

Yields 4 servings

2 tablespoons extra-virgin olive oil
2 ounces firm tofu, sliced into small strips
1 small carrot, peeled and diced
½ cup diced broccoli florets
¼ cup diced baby bella mushrooms
½ medium zucchini, diced
1 teaspoon coconut aminos
¼ teaspoon garlic powder
⅛ teaspoon ground ginger
1 cup vegetable stock

1. In a large skillet over medium-high heat, heat oil. Add tofu and stir-fry about 5 minutes until brown.

2. Add vegetables, coconut aminos, garlic powder, ginger, and stock. Bring to a boil, then stir-fry 5–7 minutes until all vegetables are cooked and tender.

3. Allow to cool, then fork-mash to desired consistency. Serve warm.

TYPES OF TOFU

Tofu comes in many varieties: silken or soft, firm, and extra-firm. When following a tofu recipe, pay attention to the type of tofu it calls for. Silken tofu is best for puddings and dips, while stir-fries mostly use firm tofu.

PEAR AND POMEGRANATE DESSERT

Pomegranates may not be easy to find as whole fruit, but you may be able to find the pomegranate seeds, which are the edible parts of the fruit and all that is needed for this recipe. Pomegranates add additional fiber, zinc, and vitamin C, and they are known for having anti-inflammatory properties and other benefits.

Yields 1 serving

1 medium Bartlett pear, peeled, cored, and chopped
¼ cup pomegranate arils
2 teaspoons plant-based butter
¼ teaspoon ground cinnamon
2 teaspoons pure maple syrup

1. Preheat oven to 350°F.

2. Combine all ingredients in an 8" × 8" baking dish. Bake 30 minutes until pear is fork-tender.

3. Allow to cool, then fork-mash to desired consistency. Serve warm.

BAKED APPLE

This classic dessert will appeal to everyone, especially baby. The cinnamon bakes right inside of the apple, a nice change from slicing the fruit and mixing it with spice.

Yields 1 serving

1 medium Honeycrisp apple
⅛ teaspoon ground cinnamon
¼ cup water

1. Preheat oven to 350°F.

2. Remove the top and core of apple, leaving it intact.

3. Sprinkle cinnamon inside apple. Pour water into a small baking dish; place apple in baking dish.

4. Bake about 45 minutes until apple is completely cooked.

5. When cooled, fork-mash to desired consistency. If preferred, the entire skin can be removed once apple is cooked. Serve immediately.

BAKED ZUCCHINI

Pizza, pizza—not quite! This recipe resembles pizza, but it's a healthier alternative in disguise without the cheese.

1 large zucchini, trimmed and sliced into ¼" rounds

½ cup canned tomato sauce

¼ teaspoon garlic powder

1 teaspoon finely chopped fresh basil

¼ teaspoon dried oregano

1 teaspoon diced yellow onion

1 tablespoon oil

1. Preheat oven to 350°F.

2. Place zucchini in a medium baking dish.

3. In a small bowl, combine tomato sauce with remaining ingredients, except for the oil. Smother zucchini with tomato sauce mixture and drizzle with oil.

4. Cover and bake 30–40 minutes until zucchini is very tender. Cool 5 minutes.

5. Take a portion for serving and fork-mash to desired consistency. Serve warm.

GOOD OLD-FASHIONED OATMEAL

This is a basic recipe for preparing rolled oats. At the first and second stages of eating, oats were ground into a powder, but now baby can enjoy oatmeal without the need for the blender! Add flavor to this recipe by incorporating any of your previously frozen fruit purées and a dab of plant-based butter for wholesome goodness. Substitute whole milk for the water if you wish.

2 cups water

1 cup old-fashioned oats (not quick-cooking)

1. In a medium saucepan over medium-high heat, bring water to a boil.

2. Add oats, reduce heat to medium-low, and simmer, stirring occasionally, 5–10 minutes until water is absorbed and oats are tender. Serve warm.

CHILLED CARROT CAKE PURÉE

This purée has all the flavors of a carrot cake but without the added sugar and animal products. Serve it chilled for a delicious treat.

Yields 3 servings

1 cup Carrot Purée (see recipe in Chapter 4)
1 tablespoon chopped raisins
1 tablespoon crushed pineapple
¼ teaspoon ground cinnamon
⅛ teaspoon ground ginger
1 teaspoon coconut oil

1. In a medium saucepan over medium heat, add all ingredients. Stir to combine.

2. Cook about 10 minutes until heated through.

3. Transfer mixture to a medium covered bowl. Refrigerate 1 hour. Serve chilled.

HIDE-AND-SEEK CAULIFLOWER MASH

Here's a great game to play with your baby over mealtime: Find the cauliflower! It's buried in there somewhere! Add 1 cup organic baby spinach to this dish for a boost of extra vitamins, minerals, and fiber.

Yields 10 servings

2 large red-skinned potatoes, chopped
1 cup water
1 medium head cauliflower, trimmed and cut into florets
1 cup oat milk
1 tablespoon extra-virgin olive oil

1. In a medium saucepan over medium-high heat, combine potatoes with enough water to cover. Bring to a boil and cook 15 minutes until soft. Drain potatoes and return to saucepan.

2. In a medium saucepan over medium-high heat, add 1 cup water and bring to a boil. Add cauliflower to a steamer insert and set into saucepan. Cover and steam 6 minutes until tender.

3. Using a slotted spoon, transfer cauliflower to saucepan with potatoes.

4. Add milk and oil. Mash with a potato masher or fork to desired consistency. Serve warm.

MASHED BLACK BEANS

Black beans provide iron, fiber, protein, and powerful antioxidants, and they're a staple for a plant-based diet. Give your baby a dose of this chunky purée a few times a week, or mix it with some of your stockpiled frozen purées to reap all the health benefits that they offer.

Yields 8 servings

1 cup dried black beans, picked through and rinsed, or 1 (15-ounce) can black beans, drained and rinsed

1 tablespoon extra-virgin olive oil

1. If using dried beans, soak them according to package directions, 6–8 hours or overnight before cooking.

2. Drain soaking water from beans and rinse.

3. In a medium saucepan over medium-low heat combine beans with enough water to cover. Bring to a simmer with the lid tilted. Cook 1–1½ hours until tender.

4. Drain and rinse cooked beans.

5. In a medium saucepan over medium-low heat, heat oil. Add cooked beans (or drained canned beans) and heat 1–2 minutes until desired temperature is reached.

6. Remove from heat and mash beans with a fork. Serve immediately.

SUPER-DUPER BLACK BEANS

Black beans contain the same amount of antioxidants as grapes and cranberries. The darker the beans, the more antioxidants they contain. Looking for an iron-rich food for your baby? Look no further than black beans. They contain almost 4 grams of iron per cup!

REFRIED PINTO BEANS

Pinto beans are a classic dish in the Southwest and Mexico. They provide the iron, fiber, and protein that your baby needs at this age. This is a basic recipe with a little flavor added. Serve mashed up alongside a serving of organic brown rice and diced tomatoes.

Yields 8 servings

1 cup dried pinto beans, picked through and rinsed, or 1 (15-ounce) can pinto beans, drained and rinsed

3–4 cups vegetable stock

1 tablespoon extra-virgin olive oil

½ medium yellow onion, peeled and finely chopped

1 clove garlic, peeled and minced

1 teaspoon cumin

1. If using dried beans, soak them according to package directions, 6–8 hours or overnight before cooking.

2. Drain soaking water from beans and rinse.

3. In a medium saucepan over medium-low heat, combine beans with enough stock to cover. Bring to a simmer with the lid tilted. Cook 1–1½ hours until tender.

4. Drain and rinse cooked beans.

5. In a medium saucepan over medium heat, heat oil. Add onion and garlic. Sauté 3–5 minutes until onion is tender.

6. Add cooked beans (or canned beans) and cumin, and cook 1–2 minutes until heated through.

7. Mash with fork. Serve warm.

VEGETABLE LASAGNA PURÉE

This recipe uses chopped lasagna noodles, which babies love. Feel free to add tofu or white beans for extra protein.

Yields 1 serving

1 cup Marinara Sauce (see recipe in this chapter)

½ cup Vegetable Stock (see recipe in Chapter 4)

1 cup chopped uncooked lasagna noodles

1. In a medium saucepan over medium-low heat, combine all ingredients. Cover and simmer 10 minutes until noodles are soft.

2. Cool slightly before serving. Serve warm.

OATMEAL WITH SAUTÉED PLANTAINS

Plantains look like giant bananas that can be found in green, yellow, or even black varieties. Green plantains are the least sweet and can be cooked and enjoyed the same way as potatoes. Yellow fruit has a mildly sweet flavor that's perfect for babies this age to enjoy, and the black plantains are super sweet and are best used for dessert. This hearty recipe makes great use of plantains and can be made for breakfast any day of the week for everyone in the family.

Yields 4 servings

1 teaspoon ground cinnamon

1 medium yellow plantain, peeled and cut into ½" pieces

1 teaspoon plant-based butter

½ cup water

¼ cup Apple Purée (see recipe in Chapter 4)

⅔ cup old-fashioned oats (not quick-cooking)

1. In a large resealable plastic bag, combine cinnamon and plantain, shaking the bag to coat thoroughly.

2. In a small skillet over medium heat, heat butter. Add plantains and cook 2 minutes on each side. Remove from heat and mash with a fork. Set aside.

3. In a small saucepan over medium-high heat, combine water and Apple Purée. Bring to a boil.

4. Stir in oats. Return to a boil.

5. Reduce heat to low and simmer about 3–5 minutes until oatmeal is of desired thickness.

6. Top oat mixture with mashed plantains and serve.

PLANTAINS VERSUS BANANAS

Plantains are firmer and have a lower sugar content than bananas. Plantains need to be cooked, but bananas are mostly eaten raw. In tropical areas of the world, plantains are often a first food for babies. Plantains are a staple item in these areas and are consumed on a daily basis.

SPINACH AND TOMATO ORZO WITH EDAMAME

This is another good pasta recipe to try with your little one. For some reason, babies really love orzo—maybe because it's cute and tiny just like them!

Yields 4 servings

½ cup chopped baby spinach
2 tablespoons mashed edamame
¼ cup prepared marinara sauce
¼ cup cooked orzo pasta
1 teaspoon Italian seasoning
1 teaspoon minced garlic

1. In a small saucepan over medium-low heat, combine all ingredients. Cover and simmer 10 minutes until heated through.

2. Remove from heat and cool slightly. Serve warm.

PEAR–GREEN BEAN BLEND
(PICTURED)

Make sure to choose beans at their peak (or frozen) for mashing. Stay away from extra-large beans, which may be tough and hard to mash, and avoid beans with blemishes or bad spots altogether.

Yields 3 servings

1 medium pear, peeled, cored, and coarsely chopped
½ cup trimmed green beans
1 teaspoon plant-based butter
½ teaspoon minced garlic
⅛ teaspoon ground ginger
1 cup water

1. In a medium saucepan over medium-low heat, combine all ingredients and simmer for 15 minutes until pears and beans are tender. Remove from heat and cool slightly.

2. Transfer to a small bowl and fork-mash ingredients together. Serve warm.

POTATO PARSNIPPETS

Yukon Gold potatoes offer an unsalted buttery-rich flavor and creamy texture. Remember to get medium-sized parsnips for better flavor.

Yields 6 servings

4 medium Yukon Gold potatoes**, peeled and chopped**
2 medium parsnips, peeled and chopped
1 tablespoon extra-virgin olive oil
¼ teaspoon salt

1. In a medium saucepan over medium-high heat, combine potatoes and parsnips with enough water to cover.

2. Bring to a boil, reduce heat to medium-low, and cook about 10–15 minutes until vegetables are tender.

3. Drain, reserving cooking liquid.

4. Return vegetables to saucepan. Mash with a potato masher or fork, then stir in oil and salt.

5. Add reserved water a little at a time until mash is desired consistency. Serve warm.

SAUTÉED SPINACH WITH GARLIC

Although it may seem like a lot of spinach in the pan, the spinach will shrink as it cooks down. Babies love the spinach and garlic combination! Spinach has a *lot* of nutrients, including protein; vitamins A, B, C, E, and K; calcium; iron; and omega-3 fatty acids. Whenever you want to add something green to your base purées, add a handful of spinach.

Yields 4 servings

1 tablespoon extra-virgin olive oil
2 cloves garlic, peeled and pressed
½ tablespoon plant-based butter
6 cups baby spinach

1. In a large skillet over medium heat, heat oil. Add garlic and butter and sauté about 20 seconds until garlic is fragrant, being careful not to burn it. Add spinach and cook 1 minute, stirring frequently.

2. Transfer spinach to a blender and pulse to a chunky purée, or fork-mash if desired. Serve immediately.

APPLE, CHERRY, AND KALE PURÉE

Kale can have a strong flavor, but the apples and cherries add just enough sweetness to balance that. Kale is a nutritious leafy green that's an excellent source of vitamin K, which helps blood to clot, as well as vitamins A and C. Kale has iron, calcium, potassium, and magnesium. To make it even more satisfying, serve with mashed potatoes.

Yields 1 serving

1 cup chopped apples
½ cup pitted cherries
½ cup kale leaves
¼ cup water

1. In a medium saucepan over medium-low heat, combine all ingredients. Simmer 20 minutes until kale and apples are very soft.

2. Transfer to a food processor and process until a semi-chunky consistency is reached. Serve warm.

VEGETABLES AND WILD RICE PURÉE

Wild rice is known to boost immunity and heart health, optimize digestion, and prevent many chronic diseases. This recipe adds lots of vegetables for flavor. It's important to add vegetables as often as you can when raising a tiny herbivore!

Yields 4 servings

¼ cup uncooked wild rice
2 teaspoons plant-based butter
¼ cup diced zucchini
¼ cup chopped yellow onion
¼ cup grated carrot

1. Cook rice according to package directions. Set aside.

2. In a small skillet over medium heat, add butter, zucchini, onion, and carrot. Cook 5 minutes until vegetables are tender.

3. Add rice to the skillet. Stir to combine. Serve if the texture is okay for your baby to chew. Otherwise, transfer rice mixture to a food processor and pulse to achieve desired consistency.

BRING ON THE FLAVOR

Add chopped fresh parsley and thyme for extra flavor and antioxidants. Toss them into the food processor before puréeing.

CHAI OVERNIGHT OATS

These sweet and spicy overnight oats are just as nutritious as the others, and have a unique flavor that will change things up a bit for your baby. You can refrigerate leftovers up to 2 days.

Yields 4 servings

½ cup old-fashioned oats (not quick-cooking)

1 teaspoon chia seeds

¼ cup Apple Purée (see recipe in Chapter 4)

1 cup unsweetened almond-cashew milk

⅛ teaspoon ground cardamom

⅛ teaspoon ground cinnamon

⅛ teaspoon ground nutmeg

⅛ teaspoon ground ginger

1. Combine all ingredients in a small Mason jar. Stir well.

2. Cover with the lid. Refrigerate overnight.

3. Stir mixture before serving.

ORANGE, BEETS, AND BANANA PURÉE

This bright and flavorful purée is so delicious, no one would know there are beets and carrots blended in. Blending beets with other fruits is a great way to ensure your baby is getting a serving of powerful antioxidants. Use prepared beets for a purée that whips up in no time!

Yields 4 servings

¼ cup chopped store-bought cooked red beets

3 tablespoons orange juice

1 medium frozen banana

¼ cup chopped carrots, steamed and cooled

Combine all ingredients in a food processor and purée until a chunky consistency is reached. Serve immediately.

AIR FRYER ZUCCHINI NUGGETS

These air fryer nuggets are crispy and delicious and one of our favorite things to eat. The seasoned chickpea flour adds a really nice "chicken" flavor. You would never know you were eating zucchini.

Yields 4 servings

¼ cup chickpea flour

¼ teaspoon garlic powder

¼ teaspoon onion powder

⅛ teaspoon salt

⅛ teaspoon ground black pepper

¼ teaspoon smoked paprika

3 tablespoons water

1 medium zucchini, trimmed and cut into ½" pieces

½ cup panko bread crumbs

1. In a medium bowl, combine flour, garlic powder, onion powder, salt, pepper, paprika, and water. Set aside.

2. Dredge one zucchini piece in flour mixture, using a spoon to coat all sides. Continue with remaining pieces.

3. Arrange nuggets in a single layer in the air fryer. Cook on 400°F for 5 minutes until golden brown. Serve immediately.

COOKING TIP

If you don't have an air fryer, you can cook these nuggets in the oven. Preheat the oven to 400°F and bake the nuggets 10–12 minutes until golden brown.

COCONUT MILK OVERNIGHT OATS

After these oats have soaked overnight, you can add more fresh fruit like chopped banana or apples for extra texture and nutrition. If your baby really enjoys this recipe, make a few jars of just the oats, cinnamon, and chia to keep in your pantry. Then, all you need to do is add the milk, set it in the fridge overnight, and boom! Breakfast is ready to go. Leftovers will keep refrigerated up to 2 days.

Yields 4 servings

½ cup old-fashioned oats (not quick-cooking)

½ teaspoon ground cinnamon

1 teaspoon chia seeds

1 cup unsweetened carton vanilla coconut milk

1. Combine all ingredients in a small Mason jar. Stir well.

2. Cover with the lid. Refrigerate overnight.

3. Stir mixture before serving.

TROPICAL NICE CREAM

(PICTURED)

This is a super easy way to make dairy-free soft-serve ice cream that is healthy and delicious! It uses the sweetness of the fruit and maple syrup to make a tasty treat. You will need to freeze the banana prior to making.

Yields 8 servings

1 (13.6-ounce) can unsweetened coconut milk

1 (12-ounce) bag frozen pineapple

1 medium frozen banana, broken into large pieces

1. Open the can of coconut milk (do not shake it first!). Skim the cream from the top and place in a food processor, reserving the remaining coconut water for another use.

2. Add pineapple and banana. Process 5–7 minutes until all banana and pineapple chunks are smooth.

3. Using a spoon, check for any large pieces. Continue processing if large pieces remain. When mixture is completely smooth, transfer to a freezer-safe container. Refrigerate 1 hour before serving cold.

BLUEBERRY-MANGO CEREAL MIX

Spruce up plain store-bought cereal by adding extra nutrition with dried fruit. You can substitute other dried fruits like apples or bananas for the blueberries and mango. Serve this as a finger-food snack, and, as your child gets older, you can serve it in a bowl with milk.

Yields 16 servings

2 cups cinnamon whole-wheat cereal, such as Cascadian Farm Organic Cinnamon Crunch

2 cups puffed rice cereal, such as Arrowhead Mills brand

2 cups dried blueberries

½ cup chopped dried mango pieces

1. In a medium bowl, combine all ingredients. Serve immediately.

2. Store leftovers in an airtight container up to 3 months.

BLUEBERRIES AND HERBS

Blueberries are a nutritional powerhouse loaded with nutrients and antioxidants, but let's not forget about the power of herbs. Parsley boasts many health benefits too as an amazing source of vitamins C and K. It's also unnoticeable in purées, so add it in!

Yields 4 servings

2 tablespoons unsweetened canned coconut milk

½ cup blueberries

2 tablespoons chopped fresh parsley

1. In a medium saucepan over medium heat, add all ingredients. Cover and cook 5 minutes, stirring occasionally until blueberries start to bubble.

2. Using a slotted spoon, transfer ingredients to a food processor. Purée until a semi-chunky consistency is reached. Serve immediately.

HOW TO NATURALLY SWEETEN TART PURÉES

If your purées are too sour or bitter for your baby to enjoy, sweeten things up by adding mashed banana or dates, or a little agave nectar or maple syrup. Remember to avoid adding honey at all costs for babies under 12 months old.

STRAWBERRY-FLAXSEED PURÉE

This purée has a wealth of vitamins C and A to keep your baby's immune system humming in full gear, defending against free radicals. The flaxseed delivers brain-supportive omega-3s and fiber. Feel free to swap the flaxseed for chia seeds for equally nutritious benefits.

Yields 4 servings

½ cup hulled strawberries
½ medium frozen banana
½ cup baby spinach
1 tablespoon ground flaxseeds
½ cup unsweetened carton coconut milk

Combine all ingredients in a food processor. Pulse until semi-smooth. Serve immediately.

BLUEBERRY OVERNIGHT OATS

Not only are overnight oats easy to make, but preparing them in a Mason jar also makes them easy to take along so that your baby can have breakfast anywhere. This recipe introduces almond-cashew milk. Make sure your pediatrician gives the thumbs-up before using the almond-cashew blend if your family has a history of nut allergies. You can also substitute any other plant-based milk such as oat milk. You can refrigerate leftovers up to 2 days.

Yields 4 servings

½ cup old-fashioned oats (not quick-cooking)
1 teaspoon chia seeds
¼ cup mashed blueberries
1 cup unsweetened almond-cashew milk

1. Combine all ingredients in a small Mason jar. Stir well.

2. Cover with the lid. Refrigerate overnight.

3. Stir mixture before serving.

ARE CASHEWS SAFE FOR BABIES?

The American Academy of Pediatrics claims that there is no current evidence to support delaying the introduction of allergenic foods, including nuts. If your baby hasn't had any allergic reactions to foods given thus far, and doesn't have a family history of food allergies, it's likely safe to offer. However, if your baby has had some allergic reactions and there is a family history of food allergies, talk to your pediatrician before introducing cashew products.

AVOCADO SMOOTHIE BOWL
(PICTURED)

This thick, rich purée is like a beginner smoothie bowl with a colorful swirl and a chia topping for a lovely presentation. It doesn't skip on taste and nutrition either. This recipe has some serious health benefits, and when you add spirulina to the mix, you're adding more protein, iron, potassium, and calcium.

Yields 8 servings

¼ cup raspberries
1 medium avocado, pitted and peeled
2 tablespoons fresh lime juice
½ medium banana, peeled
1 cup unsweetened carton coconut milk
½ teaspoon spirulina powder
1 teaspoon chia seeds

1. Add raspberries to a food processor and purée until smooth. Transfer to a small bowl and set aside. Rinse out the food processor.

2. Add avocado, lime juice, banana, milk, and spirulina to the food processor. Purée until thick and smooth.

3. Transfer avocado mixture to a serving bowl and, using a knife, swirl in raspberry purée. Sprinkle chia seeds on top. Serve immediately.

CARAMELIZED PEAR MASH

This simple yet tasty and healthy desert boasts healthy monounsaturated fat with a subtle coconut flavor and a comforting aroma in the kitchen.

Yields 6 servings

2 teaspoons extra-virgin coconut oil
2 medium Bartlett pears, peeled, cored, and sliced
2 teaspoons pure maple syrup
½ teaspoon ground cinnamon

1. In a large skillet over medium-high heat, heat oil. Add pears, maple syrup, and cinnamon. Cover and cook 10 minutes until pears are tender enough for mashing.

2. Uncover and cook an additional 3 minutes. Remove from heat and mash with a fork until pieces are small enough for your baby to chew. Serve warm or cold.

CAULIFLOWER COLCANNON

This recipe is a twist on the traditional Irish colcannon, which uses savoy cabbage, along with animal-based ingredients. This plant-based baby version includes all the flavor without sacrificing taste and nutrition. You can substitute oat milk for the almond milk if you wish.

Yields 4 servings

1 cup cauliflower florets

1 small Yukon Gold potato, peeled and cut into large pieces

⅓ cup unsweetened almond milk

½ teaspoon nutritional yeast

1 teaspoon extra-virgin olive oil

1 tablespoon plant-based butter

1 clove garlic, peeled and minced

1 cup chopped kale

1 tablespoon finely chopped green onions

1. In a medium saucepan, combine cauliflower and potato with just enough water to cover. Boil 5 minutes.

2. Using a slotted spoon, transfer vegetables to a food processor. Add milk and yeast and blend until smooth. Transfer to a medium bowl and set aside.

3. In a medium saucepan over medium heat, heat oil and butter. Add garlic, kale, and onions. Cook about 5 minutes until kale is wilted.

4. Top cauliflower blend with kale mixture. Serve warm.

CHERRIES AND BANANA PURÉE WITH A HINT OF LIME

Choose a ripe banana with some brown spots, but not one that is overly ripened. The sweetness from a more ripened banana versus one that is greenish yellow will help to cut the tartness of the lime juice, which itself helps keep the bananas from oxidizing.

Yields 2 servings

½ cup pitted cherries

1 medium banana, peeled

3 teaspoons fresh lime juice

Combine all ingredients in a food processor. Pulse two to three times to achieve a chunky, coarsely mashed texture. Serve immediately.

BUTTERNUT SQUASH AND BROWN RICE DINNER

This rice dinner is complete with a healthy serving of vegetables and complex carbohydrates. Feel free to swap the rice for quinoa or serve a combination.

Yields 6 servings

2 teaspoons plant-based butter
¼ cup chopped yellow onion
1 clove garlic, peeled and minced
1 teaspoon chopped fresh parsley
½ cup chopped baby bella mushrooms
1½ cups cubed butternut squash
½ cup vegetable stock
¼ cup cooked brown rice

1. In a medium saucepan over medium heat, warm butter. Add onion, garlic, parsley, and mushrooms, and sauté 3 minutes.

2. Add squash and stock. Reduce heat to medium-low and simmer about 5 minutes until squash is tender.

3. Add squash mixture and cooked rice to a food processor. Pulse a few times to combine.

4. Serve warm.

CAULIFLOWER WITH LEMON SAUCE

Save time by purchasing frozen riced cauliflower to make this yummy, lemony recipe. There is no need for any equipment, as all the hard work has been done!

Yields 6 servings

1 tablespoon plant-based butter
¼ cup fresh lemon juice
¼ cup vegetable stock
1 cup riced cauliflower
1 teaspoon dried parsley

1. In a medium saucepan over medium heat, warm butter, lemon juice, and stock until bubbly. Add cauliflower.

2. Reduce heat to low, cover, and simmer 15 minutes until cauliflower is tender. Garnish with dried parsley. Remove from heat and cool slightly. Serve warm.

AVOCADO, CORN, AND RED PEPPER PURÉE

The avocado pairs well with the corn and red pepper in this purée. The corn and peppers add texture for your baby at this stage while he's learning to chew. This purée can also be used as a chunky dip for crackers or toast.

Yields 4 servings

1 tablespoon extra-virgin olive oil
2 cloves garlic, peeled and chopped
¼ cup diced red bell pepper
½ cup corn kernels
¼ cup mashed avocado
⅛ teaspoon salt
⅛ teaspoon ground black pepper

1. In a medium skillet over medium heat, heat oil. Add garlic, bell pepper, and corn and stir until combined. Sauté about 5 minutes until heated through.

2. Transfer mixture to a food processor and pulse to achieve a chunky purée. Add water as needed to thin.

3. Transfer the mixture to a medium bowl. Fold in avocado and add salt and pepper. Serve warm.

CILANTRO AND LIME CHICKPEA RICE

This is a flavorful rice with a southwestern flare that uses chickpea "rice," a super healthy alternative to traditional brown rice. This meal is also delicious mixed with black beans and mashed avocado.

Yields 8 servings

1 cup uncooked chickpea rice
3 teaspoons fresh lime juice
¼ teaspoon chopped fresh cilantro
1 tablespoon plant-based butter

1. Prepare rice according to package directions.

2. Add lime juice, cilantro, and butter. Stir until combined. Serve warm.

CRANBERRY, PINEAPPLE, AND SWEET POTATO PURÉE

If you haven't tried pineapple with sweet potatoes and cranberries, you've been missing out. The pineapple adds an unexpected yet pleasing flavor and many nutritional perks. Pineapples are loaded with vitamins C and A as well as calcium, phosphorus, and a good amount of fiber too.

1 cup mashed sweet potatoes
¼ cup fresh cranberries
1 tablespoon crushed pineapple
1 teaspoon coconut oil

1. In a medium saucepan over medium heat, combine all ingredients. Cook the mixture about 10 minutes until cranberries are bubbly.

2. Stir to combine. Allow to cool and serve warm.

CREAM OF BROCCOLI PURÉE

Who says you can't make creamy meals on a plant-based diet? Here is a creamy purée that uses coconut milk instead of dairy and still tastes great! You can also substitute oat milk and it will come out just as fantastic.

Yields 8 servings

1 tablespoon plant-based butter
¼ cup sliced shallots
¼ cup sliced celery
3 cups chopped broccoli florets
¼ teaspoon dried thyme
2 cups vegetable stock
1 cup unsweetened carton coconut milk

1. In a small saucepan over medium heat, heat butter. Add shallots and celery and sauté 5 minutes.

2. Add broccoli, thyme, stock, and milk. Cover, reduce heat to medium-low, and simmer 10 minutes.

3. Transfer mixture to a food processor and pulse until a chunky texture is reached. Serve immediately.

CUCUMBER-MELON CHILLER

The riper the melon, the easier the mash! Make sure the melon you pick is ripe and flowing with juices so that mashing is a breeze. You can also use cantaloupe for this recipe, but honeydew pairs exceptionally well with the cucumbers.

Yields 1 serving

2 tablespoons diced English cucumber

2 tablespoons mashed honeydew melon

⅓ cup vanilla coconut milk yogurt alternative

In a small bowl, combine all ingredients. Serve immediately.

SOUTHWEST CORN
(PICTURED)

This south-of-the-border side dish has lots of colorful vegetables that can be picked up and eaten. When corn is in season, simply take a knife and cut the kernels from the cob vertically to remove them. Serve with a chopped salad and a side of black beans.

Yields 4 servings

1 tablespoon extra-virgin olive oil

2 cloves garlic, peeled and chopped

¼ cup diced red bell pepper

¼ cup diced green bell pepper

1 cup corn kernels

1 tablespoon chopped fresh cilantro

¼ teaspoon smoked paprika

¼ teaspoon ground cumin

⅛ teaspoon salt

⅛ teaspoon ground black pepper

In a medium skillet over medium heat, heat oil. Add all ingredients and stir until combined. Cook about 5 minutes until heated through. Serve warm.

KALE, APPLE, AND DATE PURÉE

This nutritional powerhouse purée includes many nutrients and antioxidants with anti-inflammatory and anti-aging qualities, as well as the ability to reduce the risk of cancer. Kale has become a regular leafy green staple because of all the nutrition it provides, including vitamin K.

Yields 2 servings

½ cup chopped kale
1 cup chopped apples
¼ cup water
2 medium dates, pitted

1. In a medium saucepan over medium-low heat, combine all ingredients. Simmer 20 minutes until kale and apples are very soft.

2. Transfer all ingredients to a food processor and process until semi-smooth. Serve warm.

BANANA AND KALE PURÉE WITH A HINT OF ORANGE

The sweetness of the banana offsets the natural bitterness of the kale in this purée while still providing an array of powerful nutrients in every bite. There is no need to cook the kale in this recipe. Just blend and serve!

Yields 2 servings

½ medium banana, peeled
½ cup kale leaves
2 segments medium mandarin orange

Transfer all ingredients to a food processor and process until semi-smooth. Serve immediately.

ONLY THE LEAVES

When using kale in baby purées, choose curly kale and always tear the leaves from the stem. Cooking the kale with the stem is not ideal, as it can sometimes be too tough and fibrous for babies. If you purchase kale already washed and ready to enjoy from a bag, you'll still need to tear the leaves, as most of the prepared bags still contain stems.

HERBED EGGPLANT AND ZUCCHINI

This sauté is great combined with heartier foods such as potatoes, quinoa, or any pasta. Feel free to serve it with either of those healthy carbohydrates to add more calories to the dish.

Yields 8 servings

1 teaspoon extra-virgin olive oil
½ cup cubed eggplant
½ cup cubed zucchini
2 tablespoons chopped yellow onion
¼ teaspoon dried basil
1 clove garlic, peeled and diced
¼ teaspoon dried oregano

1. In a medium skillet over medium heat, heat oil. Add remaining ingredients and sauté about 7 minutes until eggplant is brown and tender and zucchini is translucent.

2. Transfer mixture to a food processor. Pulse to combine into a chunky purée. Add water, a little at a time, to thin if needed. Serve warm.

ZUCCHINI, MANGO, AND FLAXSEED PURÉE

Zucchini's mild flavor makes it a delightful pairing in baby purées. This purée uses golden ground flaxseed meal, which gives it a nutty flavor and a healthy boost of fiber and iron.

Yields 4 servings

1 cup water
1 cup coarsely chopped zucchini
½ cup cubed mango
2 teaspoons golden flaxseed meal

1. In a medium saucepan over medium-high heat, add water and bring to a boil. Add zucchini to a steamer insert and set into saucepan. Cover and steam 3 minutes.

2. Using a slotted spoon, transfer zucchini to a food processor. Add mango and flaxseed meal. Purée until a semi-smooth consistency is reached. Serve immediately.

MANGO SURPRISE WITH CAULIFLOWER

Surprise! No one will know there is cauliflower in this purée. This recipe uses previously cooked cauliflower, which supports a healthy digestive tract.

Yields 3 servings

½ cup coarsely chopped mango
¼ cup blueberries
½ cup chilled cooked cauliflower

Place all ingredients in a food processor and blend until a semi-smooth consistency is reached. Serve immediately.

MANGO AND RASPBERRY PURÉE WITH A HINT OF LIME

(PICTURED)

Super refreshing and colorful, this purée adds a touch of lime for a little zest! Limes are a good source of vitamin C and antioxidants that protect your cells from harm.

Yields 2 servings

½ cup raspberries
1 cup coarsely chopped mango
1 teaspoon fresh lime juice
2 teaspoons agave nectar

Combine all ingredients in a food processor. Pulse two to three times to achieve a chunky, coarsely mashed texture. Serve immediately.

EDAMAME, PEAR, AND OATS PURÉE

Here is something you can whip up using items you have on hand. Alternatively, use any previously frozen purées to make this a purée packed with protein and antioxidants.

Yields 2 servings

2 tablespoons mashed edamame
2 tablespoons mashed pear
¼ cup Good Old-Fashioned Oatmeal (see recipe in this chapter)
1 teaspoon orange juice

In a small bowl, combine all ingredients. Serve warm.

MINTY PINEAPPLE AND PEACH PURÉE

Fresh and minty, this purée is overflowing with vitamin C, which helps keep immune systems strong and also helps reduce inflammation. Giving your baby plenty of greens that taste good will help him associate greens with yummy flavors and encourage him to be a vegetable lover over time.

Yields 3 servings

½ cup frozen peaches
¼ cup canned crushed pineapple
¼ cup chopped baby spinach
3 fresh mint leaves

Combine all the ingredients in a food processor. Pulse to combine into a chunky consistency. Serve chilled.

GINGER, ORANGE, AND CARROT MASH

The flavors of ginger and orange give carrots a makeover in this purée. Vegetables can be flavored with many different herbs and spices that are appealing to beginning plant-based eaters.

Yields 4 servings

4 medium carrots, peeled and cut into 1" rounds

⅛ teaspoon ground ginger

2 teaspoons plant-based butter

¼ cup orange juice

1. In a medium saucepan over medium heat, add all ingredients. Cook 10 minutes until carrots are fork-tender.

2. Remove from heat. Mash with a fork or cut into bite-sized pieces for your baby to self-feed. Serve warm.

HERBED CARROT AND PARSNIP PURÉE

This is a wonderfully flavored root vegetable purée that really adds punch to carrots and parsnips. Take advantage of the herbs in your garden and use them to flavor your purées.

1. In a medium saucepan over medium heat, add all ingredients. Cook 15–20 minutes until vegetables are fork-tender.

2. Remove from heat. Mash with a fork or cut into bite-sized pieces for your baby to self-feed. Serve warm.

Yields 4 servings

2 medium parsnips, peeled and cut into large pieces

2 medium carrots, peeled and cut into large pieces

1 teaspoon chopped fresh dill

1 teaspoon chopped fresh rosemary

2 teaspoons plant-based butter

¼ cup vegetable stock or water

STRAWBERRY AND ASPARAGUS BITES

Asparagus helps fight free radicals and destroy carcinogens. It provides an abundance of folic acid and is a great source of fiber, magnesium, calcium, potassium, and antioxidants.

Yields 1 serving

1 large strawberry, hulled and chopped into bite-sized pieces

1 medium asparagus spear, steamed and chopped into bite-sized pieces

In a small bowl, toss together strawberry and asparagus. Serve immediately.

SWEET POTATOES WITH APRICOT GLAZE
(PICTURED)

Who needs the oven when you can easily whip up a pot of delicious sweet potatoes on the stovetop? Sweet potatoes pack a lot of beta-carotene, and, coupled with the healthy dose of fat from the coconut oil or plant-based butter, your little one will surely be satisfied.

Yields 6 servings

2 large sweet potatoes, peeled and cut into 2" pieces

⅓ cup water

1 tablespoon coconut oil or plant-based butter

½ teaspoon ground cinnamon

1 teaspoon apricot preserves

1. In a medium saucepan over medium heat, add sweet potatoes, water, oil or butter, and cinnamon. Stir to combine.

2. Cover and cook 15–20 minutes until sweet potatoes fall apart when pierced with a fork or they've reached desired consistency.

3. Transfer potatoes to a medium bowl and, using a fork or potato masher, mash to achieve desired consistency.

4. Top a serving with apricot preserves. Swirl preserves into sweet potatoes with a spoon. Serve immediately.

OATS AND QUINOA BREAKFAST

This breakfast is great on its own and is full of nutrients. Top it with Skillet Apple Mash (see recipe in Chapter 7) for an irresistible breakfast that your little one will devour. You can substitute oat milk for the coconut milk if you prefer.

Yields 4 servings

¼ cup old-fashioned oats (not quick-cooking)
¼ cup quinoa
1 cup unsweetened carton coconut milk, plus more for thinning
1 tablespoon ground golden flaxseeds
½ medium banana, peeled and mashed

1. In a small saucepan over medium heat, combine oats, quinoa, and milk. Bring to a boil.

2. Reduce the heat to low, cover, and simmer 10–15 minutes until oats and quinoa are soft and creamy.

3. Stir in flaxseeds and banana. Add additional milk to thin if needed. Serve warm.

QUINOA AND DATES

Quinoa is the perfect base for making baby food because it is a complete source of protein and is a standout among other grains. Quinoa and dates also make a harmonious pairing because of the fiber content and disease-fighting antioxidants.

Yields 1 serving

¼ cup cooked quinoa, cooled
1 tablespoon finely chopped dates
¼ cup oat milk
⅛ teaspoon ground cinnamon

1. In a medium saucepan over medium heat, combine all ingredients. Cook 5 minutes until heated through, stirring occasionally. If you feel the mixture is a good consistency at this point, you can skip the next step and serve.

2. Transfer all ingredients to a food processor and pulse to achieve desired consistency. Serve warm.

SPINACH, ARTICHOKE, AND CHICKPEA PURÉE

Artichokes are loaded with a long list of nutrients. They are a great source of vitamins C and K as well as folate and magnesium. Give them a try in this purée, and if it goes well, you have another power plant in your arsenal to combine with other purées.

Yields 1 serving

2 medium artichoke hearts
¼ cup canned chickpeas, drained and rinsed
¼ cup baby spinach
½ teaspoon extra-virgin olive oil

Add all ingredients to a food processor. Pulse to achieve desired consistency. Add water to thin, if necessary. Serve immediately.

STRAWBERRY AND DATE MASH

If your little one isn't too fond of dates, try mashing them with strawberries. The strawberries add a bright flavor and enhance the taste of the dates. This dish can also be used as a sweetener with foods such as unsweetened plant-based yogurt, rice, or oatmeal.

Yields 6 servings

¼ cup pitted dates
1 cup sliced strawberries

1. Add dates to a medium bowl. Pour in enough boiling water to cover and allow to soak 3–4 hours until they are completely hydrated and soft.

2. Combine strawberries with dates in a food processor. Pulse until mixture has a chunky texture. Serve immediately.

THAI COCONUT-VEGETABLE PURÉE

Baby purées can be inspired from any cuisine, and this is an example of one of them. Thai meals aren't just for the grown-ups—your little ones can have a sampling of them too. You can serve this as a soup by skipping the purée step if your baby can gum the softened vegetables. If you've been given the okay from your pediatrician to offer peanut butter, you can add a tablespoon for extra flavor.

Yields 6 servings

2 tablespoons extra-virgin coconut oil
½ cup cubed (½" pieces) tofu
1 clove garlic, peeled and chopped
¼ cup chopped celery
¼ cup chopped yellow onion
¼ cup chopped red bell pepper
⅛ teaspoon ground ginger
¾ cup unsweetened canned coconut milk
¼ cup sweet peas
1 teaspoon chopped fresh cilantro
2 cups Vegetable Stock (see recipe in Chapter 4)

1. In a large saucepan over medium-high heat, heat oil. Add tofu, garlic, celery, onion, pepper, and ginger. Sauté, stirring occasionally, 5 minutes until onion is translucent. Add milk and peas. Bring to a boil.

2. Reduce heat to low and simmer 10 minutes, stirring occasionally. Stir in cilantro.

3. Transfer mixture to a food processor, add Vegetable Stock, and pulse a few times to achieve desired consistency. Serve warm.

SHAKE UP THE COCONUT MILK

When using the canned coconut milk in this recipe, make sure to shake the can very well. Other recipes may ask for just the thick and creamy coconut "cream" (fat), but for this one you'll need the fat and the water. So shake it up!

TOFU, SWEET POTATOES, AND DATES

Protein, fiber, fat, antioxidants, repeat! Babies love sweet potatoes and dates, and combining them with tofu gives this purée a hefty dose of protein. This is a great pick to serve any time of the day.

Yields 6 servings

2 medium sweet potatoes, peeled and cut into 2" pieces
½ cup water
½ (12-ounce) package silken tofu
¼ cup dates
1 teaspoon coconut oil
½ teaspoon ground cinnamon

1. In a medium saucepan over medium heat, combine potatoes and water.

2. Cover and cook 15 minutes until sweet potatoes fall apart when pierced with a fork. Remove from heat and cool 10 minutes.

3. Transfer potatoes to a food processor and add tofu, dates, oil, and cinnamon. Process to achieve desired consistency. Serve warm.

MEXICAN FIESTA RICE

Skip the store-bought packages of rice for complete control over your own. Just add salsa and nutritional yeast for a cheesy flavor to brown rice.

Yields 4 servings

¼ cup uncooked brown rice
¼ cup mild salsa
1 tablespoon nutritional yeast

1. Cook brown rice according to package directions.

2. Add salsa and nutritional yeast. Stir to combine. Serve warm.

ADD SPICE TO YOUR RICE

Add prepared salsa, dip, or dressing to quickly add some kick to your rice. For your little one you can choose a mild salsa to start. For the rest of the family, mix in a hotter salsa or add some hot sauce or fresh serrano or jalapeño peppers to increase the heat.

BANANA-CINNAMON OATMEAL

Oats are extremely inexpensive and versatile. Don't bother purchasing preflavored packs of instant oatmeal when you can make so many different oatmeal flavors using fresh ingredients. You'll have more flexibility to create flavor combinations that your child loves.

Yields 2 servings

¼ cup old-fashioned oats (not quick-cooking)
½ cup unsweetened carton coconut milk
1 teaspoon wheat germ
⅛ teaspoon ground cinnamon
½ medium banana, peeled and mashed

1. In a small saucepan over medium-high heat, combine oats, milk, wheat germ, and cinnamon. Bring to a boil. Cook, stirring, about 5 minutes until thickened.

2. Stir banana into the mixture. Serve immediately.

LOVE THY OATS

Not only are oats economical; they are also loaded with soluble fiber, antioxidants, calcium, magnesium, B vitamins, and vitamin E. Oats are famous for maintaining healthy blood-sugar levels and lowering bad cholesterol. Keep oats stored in an airtight container in a cool, dry place.

CHUNKY CHERRY APPLESAUCE

If you don't have fresh cherries on hand, you can substitute frozen cherries or even cherry preserves. If you use cherry preserves, reduce the amount to ½ cup. Leftovers of this dish can be refrigerated up to 5 days.

Yields 6 servings

5 medium Fuji or Gala apples**, peeled, cored, and chopped**

¾ cup pitted and chopped Bing or Rainier cherries

¼ cup water

1. In a medium saucepan over medium-high heat, combine all ingredients. Bring to a boil.

2. Cook, stirring occasionally, 10–15 minutes until tender.

3. Mash with a potato masher until a coarse texture is reached. For a smooth consistency, purée the mixture in a blender 30–60 seconds.

4. Serve warm or chilled.

CHERRIES ARE ALL THE RAGE

Cherries are loaded with potassium and protective antioxidants that fight against cancer. The darker and riper the cherry, the more antioxidants it contains. Load up on these ruby jewels.

MARINARA SAUCE

This simple sauce can be used with pastas or spiralized vegetables, including chickpea, black bean, or edamame. Refrigerate leftovers up to 5 days or freeze up to 1 month.

Yields 8 servings

¼ cup extra-virgin olive oil

2 cloves garlic, peeled and minced

1 small yellow onion, peeled and finely chopped

¼ cup chopped fresh flat-leaf parsley

¼ teaspoon ground black pepper

1 teaspoon dried oregano

1 teaspoon dried basil

2 (14.5-ounce) cans crushed tomatoes, drained

1 (6-ounce) can tomato paste

½ cup Vegetable Stock (see recipe in Chapter 4)

1. In a large saucepan over medium heat, heat oil. Add garlic and onion and sauté about 5 minutes until onion is translucent and fragrant.

2. Add remaining ingredients and stir well to combine.

3. Reduce heat to low and simmer 1 hour, stirring occasionally. Serve warm as a dip or pasta sauce.

BPA IN CANNED TOMATOES

Bisphenol A (BPA) is an industrial chemical used in the linings of metal cans to prevent corrosion. BPA may cause adverse health effects in infants and children. If you're concerned about BPA in canned tomatoes or other produce, look for brands that use BPA-free liners (specified on the can) or choose canned products in cartons or glass jars to avoid the issue altogether. If you are unsure if your favorite brand contains BPA, email the company directly to find out.

PEACH APPLESAUCE

Chances are you won't find organic peach applesauce at the store. This is a recipe that my kids and I created with ingredients we had on hand one day—one of the joys of making healthy organic meals from scratch! You can refrigerate leftovers up to 5 days or freeze up to 1 month.

Yields 12 servings

5 medium Fuji or Gala apples**, peeled, cored, and chopped**

1 cup chopped peaches

¼ cup water

¼ teaspoon ground cinnamon

2 tablespoons Cinnamon-Date Mash (see recipe in Chapter 5)

1 teaspoon vanilla extract

1. In a large saucepan over medium-high heat, combine all the ingredients. Bring to a boil.

2. Cook 10–15 minutes until fruit is tender, stirring occasionally.

3. Mash with a potato masher until a coarse texture is reached. For a smooth consistency, purée in a blender 30–60 seconds.

4. Serve warm or chilled.

SERIOUSLY? CANNED PEACHES ARE MORE NUTRITIOUS?

A study conducted by Oregon State University shows that canned cling peaches have more vitamin C, vitamin A, folate, and antioxidants than fresh peaches due to the canning process. So don't snub your nose at organic canned cling peaches!

7

FUN AND FINGERLICIOUS FOOD:
TRANSITIONAL MEALS FOR TODDLERS
········ **(12+ MONTHS)** ········

Your baby has gone from a little explorer to an expert adventurer! From twelve months old, your toddler can have a wide array of plant-based foods. You should incorporate five (1-ounce) servings of fruit or vegetables into your child's diet. Your child is at a stage where she may prefer one food over another and may even express that! Therefore, in order to give her all the nutrients her growing body needs, you may have to disguise fruit and vegetables by incorporating them into smoothies, pasta sauce, or baked treats. Continue to offer foods that are refused, and don't be afraid to spruce them up by adding healthy oils such as olive oil, sauces, or condiments such as no-sugar-added ketchup or mustard to them for added flavor.

The recipes in this chapter allow for self-feeding and provide your child ample practice with using eating utensils. This chapter also introduces new foods such as teething biscuits and biscotti, risotto, fruit smoothies, and vegetable pizza—which all encourage self-feeding. By this age, your child should be weaned from breast milk or formula. However, if still breastfeeding, offer breast milk as a supplement, as most of his nutrition will come from meals. It's important to make sure your child is getting enough calcium and vitamin D through calcium-rich foods and sun exposure.

You may continue serving all of the meals in previous chapters by dicing them instead of puréeing. If you still have frozen purées left in the freezer, use them in muffins or smoothies, or as dips!

FRUIT-INFUSED COCONUT MILK

This recipe infuses fruit flavors into coconut milk. Flavored coconut milk is super delicious and a healthy substitute for cow's milk. To add protein and a serving of omega-2s, add ½ teaspoon chia seeds to your child's serving and drink up!

Yields 8 servings

½ medium banana, peeled and sliced
10 large strawberries, hulled and sliced
¼ cup raspberries, halved
4 cups unsweetened carton coconut milk

1. Add all ingredients to a pitcher and stir to combine. Refrigerate overnight to allow the flavors to develop (or chill 4 hours if your child can't wait).

2. Strain fruit from milk and serve. Consume within 2 days of infusing.

SMOKY COLLARD MASH

The smoky flavor in this recipe comes from the smoked paprika. If you can't find smoked paprika, you can add a tablespoon of hickory liquid smoke. Either one adds a wonderful aroma and flavor that's irresistible. Serve this dish with a side of sweet potato cornbread with maple butter for a truly southern experience.

Yields 4 servings

4 heaping cups chopped collard greens
1 tablespoon extra-virgin olive oil
1 small yellow onion, peeled and chopped
1 clove garlic, peeled and minced
4 cups Vegetable Stock (see recipe in Chapter 4)
¼ teaspoon smoked paprika
⅛ teaspoon salt
⅛ teaspoon ground black pepper

1. In a large saucepan over medium heat, combine all ingredients and cook 25 minutes until collards are tender and bright green.

2. Add ½ cup cooked collards to a small bowl. Serve immediately. Refrigerate any leftover collards for up to 3 days.

CRUNCHY GREEN BEANS

This recipe is similar to traditional green bean casserole, but the preparation is a lot faster and the texture is crunchier.

Yields 6 servings

1 cup water
3 cups trimmed fresh green beans
3 tablespoons extra-virgin olive oil, divided
1 cup crushed corn flakes
⅛ teaspoon salt
⅛ teaspoon ground black pepper

1. In a medium saucepan over medium-high heat, add water and bring to a boil. Add beans to a steamer insert and set into saucepan. Cover and steam about 10 minutes until tender.

2. Meanwhile, in a large skillet over medium-low heat, warm 1 tablespoon oil. Add corn flakes and cook 1 minute until brown. Transfer corn flakes to a small bowl and set aside.

3. To the same skillet over medium-high heat, heat remaining 2 tablespoons oil. Add beans, salt, and pepper. Sauté 3–4 minutes until heated through.

4. Using a slotted spoon, transfer beans to a medium bowl.

5. Top beans with corn flakes (or mix together if desired) and serve.

ORZO HARMONY

It is common to mistake orzo for rice because they look like twins, but orzo is actually a pasta. It's a great choice for babies mastering the art of chewing. This dish is certainly one that guarantees your self-feeder will grab a handful.

Yields 4 servings

2 cups Vegetable Stock (see recipe in Chapter 4)

¾ cup uncooked orzo pasta

1 tablespoon plant-based butter

3 tablespoons chopped fresh flat-leaf parsley

3 tablespoons chopped fresh chives

3 tablespoons fresh lemon juice

½ cup chopped broccoli florets

1. In a small saucepan over medium-high heat, bring Vegetable Stock to a boil.

2. Add orzo and cook 5–7 minutes until al dente. Drain all but a few tablespoons of liquid to prevent pasta from sticking together.

3. In a medium mixing bowl, toss together butter, parsley, chives, lemon juice, broccoli, and orzo to coat.

4. Serve warm or cold. Refrigerate leftovers up to 3 days.

STOCK-FULL OF FLAVOR!

Consider substituting vegetable stock for plain water in savory recipes.
Not only do you boost nutritional content, but you also boost the flavor factor.
This technique is particularly useful for anything that is boiled,
like rice, pasta, or potatoes.

COOL PASTA SALAD

Pasta is a wonderful finger food for toddlers. This Cool Pasta Salad can be eaten with tiny fingers, but keep a bib handy—things can get a little messy! This pasta offers whole grains and a boatload of colorful vegetables with a ton of nutrition.

Yields 8 servings

1 cup uncooked whole-wheat rotini or mini farfalle pasta

1 tablespoon extra-virgin olive oil

1 teaspoon distilled white vinegar

2 teaspoons Italian seasoning

½ teaspoon garlic powder

¼ cup chopped broccoli florets

¼ cup diced green bell pepper

¼ cup diced red bell pepper

¼ cup grated carrot

¼ cup diced Vidalia onion

⅛ teaspoon salt

⅛ teaspoon ground black pepper

1. Cook pasta according to package directions. Rinse with cold water to stop the pasta from cooking. Drain and place in the refrigerator to cool.

2. Meanwhile, prepare dressing by whisking together oil, vinegar, Italian seasoning, and garlic powder in a small bowl. Set aside.

3. Combine pasta and prepared dressing. Stir in broccoli, bell peppers, carrot, onion, salt, and black pepper. Serve chilled. Refrigerate leftovers up to 3 days.

TOO-GOOD TOMATO SOUP

If you have a 15-ounce can of organic diced tomatoes in the pantry, you can certainly use that in place of the fresh tomatoes in this recipe. For a nutritional boost, try adding whole-wheat pasta shapes such as stars or alphabets.

Yields 6 servings

2 large tomatoes, **cored and diced**

2 tablespoons tomato paste

2½ cups Vegetable Stock (see recipe in Chapter 4)

½ teaspoon dried oregano

½ teaspoon dried basil

¼ teaspoon salt

⅛ teaspoon ground black pepper

1. In a medium saucepan over medium heat, combine all ingredients. Cover.

2. Gently bring to a boil and cook 10 minutes. Remove from heat. Let cool about 5 minutes. Serve warm.

VITAMIN-PACKED TOMATOES

Tomatoes provide vitamin C, potassium, fiber, and lycopene, which helps keep the heart and eyes healthy. The riper the tomato, the higher the levels of lycopene it contains.

LEMONY ZOODLES

Time to whip out the spiralizer to make zucchini noodles. Feel free to create any style you wish—ribbons, spaghetti, fettuccine, any one will do. If you don't have a spiralizer, you can purchase spiralized zucchini in the fresh produce section.

Yields 8 servings

2 teaspoons avocado oil
1 cup spiralized zucchini
¼ cup fresh lemon juice
2 tablespoons diced tomatoes
1 clove garlic, peeled and minced
1 teaspoon dried parsley

1. In a medium skillet over medium heat, combine oil, zucchini, lemon juice, tomatoes, and garlic. Cook 5-7 minutes until heated through. Stir in parsley.

2. Before serving, cut zoodles into smaller, chewable pieces. Serve warm.

SWAP IT

You can replace the zucchini noodles for regular whole-wheat pasta or any other plant-based pasta. Boil the pasta according to the package directions and then replace the zucchini noodles with ½ cup cooked pasta. Follow the instructions as written.

VEGETABLE COUSCOUS

Couscous is a household staple in Mediterranean countries and is usually served as a side dish. Couscous is made from granules of durum wheat and is traditionally prepared by steaming.

Yields 4 servings

1 cup Vegetable Stock (see recipe in Chapter 4)
1 cup uncooked tricolor couscous
1½ tablespoons extra-virgin olive oil
1 clove garlic, peeled and minced
1 medium green onion, trimmed and chopped
¼ cup shredded carrot
1 cup finely chopped broccoli florets

1. In a small saucepan over high heat, add Vegetable Stock. Bring to a boil. Add couscous. Cover and remove from heat. Let sit 5 minutes until Vegetable Stock is absorbed. Fluff with a fork.

2. In a medium skillet over medium heat, heat oil. Add garlic, green onion, carrot, and broccoli. Sauté until onion is softened, about 4 minutes.

3. Mix together couscous and vegetable mixture. Serve warm.

SMOTHERED ASPARAGUS

Medium-sized stalks of asparagus work best for this recipe. Sautéing them in the oil makes them tender with a little crunch for toddlers to eat, and also offers a nice serving of healthy fat.

Yields 4 servings

2 tablespoons extra-virgin olive oil
2 cloves garlic, peeled and minced
5 medium asparagus spears, trimmed
2 tablespoons Dijon mustard
⅛ teaspoon salt
⅛ teaspoon ground black pepper

1. In a medium skillet over medium heat, heat oil. Add garlic and sauté 30 seconds. Add asparagus and mustard and toss with oil to coat. Cook about 7 minutes until tender.

2. Season with salt and pepper. Cut into bite-sized pieces. Serve immediately.

ITALIAN SNOW PEAS

Super quick and simple, these crunchy snow peas are a favorite with toddlers. Make sure to remove all strings from the peas.

Yields 4 servings

1 tablespoon extra-virgin olive oil
1 clove garlic, peeled and minced
¾ teaspoon Italian seasoning
½ pound fresh snow peas, trimmed
⅛ teaspoon salt

1. In a medium skillet over medium heat, heat oil. Stir in garlic and Italian seasoning and cook about 15 seconds until fragrant.

2. Add snow peas, tossing to coat. Cook 2 minutes. Sprinkle with salt and serve warm.

KALE CHIPS

Kale has a slightly bitter flavor that may not generate happy faces from the kids when you serve it to them raw. But if you dress it up with a little flavor and add some crunch, it becomes a healthy snack that the kids can't stop eating.

Yields 5 servings

1 bunch fresh kale, stems removed
½ tablespoon extra-virgin olive oil
Pinch salt
½ teaspoon garlic powder

1. Preheat oven to 375°F.

2. Arrange kale in a single layer on a large baking sheet. Drizzle with oil and sprinkle with salt and garlic powder.

3. Bake about 10 minutes until the outer edges of the leaves turn brown. The leaves will crisp more as they stand. Serve immediately. Store in an airtight container and consume within 2 days.

FARMERS' MARKET KALE

Visit your local farmers' market for great prices on organic kale. Although many small farms are not regulated by the USDA, you can talk directly to the farmers about the use of pesticides in their methods.

HAPPY BIRTHDAY MELON "CAKE"

This easy melon "cake" is so fast to make because it doesn't require any time baking in the oven. A healthier alternative to traditional birthday cake, the vibrant colors of fruit will entice any toddler.

Yields 12 servings

1 personal-sized watermelon or ½ medium watermelon

3 cups whipped cream (optional)

3 small kiwifruit, peeled and sliced

2 medium nectarines, peeled and sliced

1 pint strawberries, hulled and halved

1. Carefully cut away the rind from watermelon slices, being careful to maintain the circle shape.

2. On a cake platter, layer one watermelon round. Spread with whipped cream and stack another round on top. Continue layering with remaining watermelon rounds and whipped cream. For a tiered look, trim each circle about 2" smaller than the previous layer (eat the leftover as you cut away—you don't want that juicy watermelon to go to waste!).

3. Arrange kiwifruit, nectarines, and strawberries on top of the watermelon any way you choose. Serve immediately.

MAKE IT PERSONAL

Personal-sized watermelons are perfect for making this beautiful watermelon cake for your child's birthday. For a more elaborate cake, grab a bigger watermelon that can serve a large crowd. Watermelon is known to have little to no traces of pesticides, so if you can't find an organic watermelon, a regular one is safe for toddlers to eat. Also for food safety purposes, it is important to wash the outside of any melon well before cutting into it.

CINNAMON-PINEAPPLE CRUMBLE

This delicious crumble can be made with all-purpose flour, or you can substitute almond flour to make it gluten-free. You can also use canned pineapple chunks, but the slices are easier for toddlers to eat.

Yields 10 servings

PINEAPPLE FILLING
2 (20-ounce) cans pineapple slices in juice, drained
½ teaspoon vanilla extract
2 tablespoons all-purpose flour

CRUMBLE TOPPING
½ cup almond flour
¼ cup raw sugar
½ teaspoon ground cinnamon
5 tablespoons cold plant-based butter

1. Preheat oven to 375°F.

2. Place pineapple slices a large bowl. Add vanilla and flour. Mix well.

3. In a food processor, combine all the Crumble Topping ingredients. Pulse until butter is crumbled and incorporated into the mixture.

4. Spoon Pineapple Filling into an ungreased 2-quart glass baking dish. Spread Crumble Topping evenly over filling.

5. Bake 45 minutes until topping is a light golden brown. Serve warm.

BANANA QUESADILLAS WITH RASPBERRY SAUCE

When your child wants something sweet, this healthy dessert will certainly satisfy his sweet tooth while providing a healthy serving of whole grains, potassium, and antioxidants.

Yields 4 servings

RASPBERRY SAUCE
¾ cup frozen raspberries, thawed
1½ tablespoons fresh lemon juice

BANANA FILLING
1 tablespoon plant-based butter
2 (8") whole-wheat flour tortillas
1 medium banana, peeled and sliced
¼ teaspoon ground cinnamon

1. Make the Raspberry Sauce by combining all ingredients in a blender. Refrigerate until ready to use.

2. Generously butter one side of each tortilla.

3. Heat a medium skillet over medium heat. Place a tortilla butter-side down in the skillet. Quickly arrange banana slices in the center, 1" from the edge. Sprinkle with cinnamon. Place the other tortilla butter-side up on top of bananas.

4. Cook quesadilla 3–4 minutes until the bottom is lightly golden. Using a large spatula, carefully flip quesadilla. Cook 3–4 minutes until lightly golden on the other side.

5. Cut into quarters with a pizza cutter. Drizzle with Raspberry Sauce. Serve immediately.

SWEET POTATO–CORNBREAD MUFFINS WITH MAPLE BUTTER

These muffins will not last long in your house. They are a nice break from regular cornbread and are the perfect-sized snack for toddlers.

Yields 12 servings

MUFFIN BATTER

1 cup all-purpose unbleached flour

⅔ cup yellow cornmeal

2 teaspoons baking powder

½ teaspoon salt

1½ cups mashed sweet potato

¼ cup honey

¼ teaspoon baking soda

⅓ cup coconut oil or plant-based butter

1 cup oat milk

MAPLE BUTTER

¼ cup plant-based butter

1 tablespoon pure maple syrup

1. Preheat oven to 400°F. Lightly grease a twelve-cup muffin pan.

2. In a medium bowl, combine flour, cornmeal, baking powder, and salt. Stir until well combined.

3. Stir in remaining Muffin Batter ingredients, being careful not to overmix.

4. Fill each prepared muffin cup about halfway. Bake about 20 minutes until a toothpick inserted in the center of a muffin comes out clean.

5. In a small bowl, combine Maple Butter ingredients. Whip with an electric hand mixer until fluffy.

6. Break the warm muffins in half and spread with Maple Butter to serve. Store remaining Maple Butter in an airtight container and refrigerate up to 1 week or freeze up to 1 month.

ON THE MOVE

Take a small lunch sack whenever you go out with your child and keep healthy snacks like these muffins on hand. Packing a snack bag is not only helpful to have in a pinch (like in unforeseen weather that brings traffic to a halt for 2 hours); it also eliminates the need to pop into a drive-through or convenience store and rely on less healthy alternatives.

AVOCADO TOAST

(PICTURED)

Any type of bread will work to make this Avocado Toast, be it gluten-free, dairy-free, sugar-free, or even homemade bread. Just be sure to read the label on store-bought bread to ensure there are no questionable ingredients and that it has a good amount of fiber and protein per slice. If desired, you can sprinkle this with a smidgen of salt and pepper.

Yields 2 servings

½ teaspoon garlic powder
1 teaspoon plant-based butter, softened
1 slice organic bread
2 tablespoons mashed avocado

1. In a small bowl, combine garlic powder and butter. Set aside.

2. Toast bread in a toaster until lightly golden. While bread is still warm, spread butter evenly on one side. Spread mashed avocado on top.

3. Cut in quarters. Serve immediately.

SAUTÉED CABBAGE

I've found the most beautiful cabbage heads at the farmers' market, with large vibrant green outer leaves. Sometimes, when you purchase cabbage at the store, the outer leaves get destroyed in the shipping process, and you're often left with only the white part of the cabbage. For the best results, buy a cabbage with all the leaves intact.

Yields 6 servings

3 tablespoons extra-virgin olive oil
½ small head green cabbage, cored and cut into thin lengthwise slices
⅛ teaspoon salt
⅛ teaspoon ground black pepper

1. In a large skillet over medium-high heat, heat oil. Add cabbage, tossing to coat.

2. Season with salt and pepper and cook, stirring occasionally, about 15–20 minutes until tender. Serve immediately.

VEGETABLE AND HUMMUS PLATTER

When the kids are playing around the house, it's nice to have a fresh vegetable platter out so they can munch here and there. Playing builds up an appetite, and having fresh vegetables available makes it easy for toddlers to grab and go.

Yields 4 servings

6 slices cucumber

6 strips red bell pepper

6 sticks celery

6 sticks carrot

½ cup prepared hummus

Arrange vegetables on a round plate. Add hummus to a small bowl and place in the center of the plate. Serve immediately.

SOUTHWEST POTATO SALAD

Here is a power-packed potato salad with black beans for fiber and protein and lots of vegetables. You can refrigerate leftovers up to 3 days.

Yields 8 servings

2 large Yukon Gold potatoes, **cut into small cubes**

½ medium red onion, peeled and chopped

¼ cup minced green bell pepper

⅓ cup fresh corn kernels

¼ cup canned black beans, drained and rinsed

2 tablespoons minced fresh chives

⅓ cup prepared mild salsa

⅛ teaspoon salt, or to taste

⅛ teaspoon ground black pepper

1. In a medium saucepan over high heat, combine potatoes with enough water to cover. Bring to a boil.

2. Reduce heat to medium-low, cover, and simmer until just fork-tender, about 15 minutes. Drain and set aside to cool completely.

3. In a large bowl, mix potatoes with remaining ingredients. Serve immediately or cover and refrigerate 1–2 hours and serve cold.

MAGIC MANGO COLESLAW

The mango gives this coleslaw a magical flavor from the tropics. For another edge on a classic side dish, substitute blueberries for the mango during their peak season to make Blueberry Coleslaw.

Yields 4 servings

2 cups shredded green or red cabbage or coleslaw mix

½ cup chopped mango

2 teaspoons chopped red onion

4 teaspoons balsamic vinegar

¼ cup honey

¼ cup vegan mayonnaise

1. In a large bowl, combine cabbage or coleslaw mix, mango, and onion. Set aside.

2. In a small bowl, combine vinegar, honey, and mayonnaise. Mix well to create a dressing.

3. Combine dressing and cabbage mixture. Toss well and serve. Refrigerate leftovers up to 3 days.

CHILLED CINNAMON-COCONUT CUSTARD

This divine eggless custard can be enjoyed warm or cold, but cold is the best! With only a handful of ingredients, it's also a breeze to prepare.

Yields 2 servings

½ teaspoon ground cinnamon

1 cup unsweetened canned coconut milk

2 teaspoons vanilla extract

2 teaspoons honey

1 teaspoon tapioca flour

1. In a small saucepan over medium heat, combine cinnamon, milk, vanilla, and honey.

2. Bring to a boil, stirring frequently. Reduce heat to medium-low and simmer 3 minutes.

3. Vigorously whisk in tapioca flour until the mixture thickens. If the mixture isn't thick enough, add another teaspoon of flour; if it's too thick, add another teaspoon milk. The mixture should resemble a soft pudding.

4. Remove from heat and allow to cool 5–10 minutes. Serve warm or chilled.

VEGETABLE QUESADILLAS

This recipe can be tailored to include your toddler's favorite vegetables and whatever plant-based lifestyle you live. You can add plant-based cheese, dairy cheese, or no cheese! Serve with your favorite hummus. Customize however you like!

Yields 2 servings

1 tablespoon plant-based butter, divided
1 (8") plant-based tortilla
⅓ cup mashed black beans
1 tablespoon diced red bell pepper
1 tablespoon diced green bell pepper
½ tablespoon diced red onion
½ teaspoon minced garlic
1 teaspoon chopped fresh cilantro
¼ cup shredded plant-based cheese

1. Generously spread ½ tablespoon butter on one side of tortilla. Spread mashed beans on the opposite side. Set aside.

2. In a medium skillet over medium heat, melt remaining ½ tablespoon butter. Add peppers, onion, and garlic. Cook until vegetables are tender, stirring frequently. Transfer into a small bowl.

3. In the same skillet over medium heat, place the tortilla, butter-side down. Quickly spoon cooked vegetables and cilantro on top of the beans. Sprinkle with cheese. Cook tortilla 3–4 minutes until the bottom is lightly golden. Fold the opposite side of the tortilla on top of vegetables and cheese. The tortilla should now resemble a half-moon. Remove from heat.

4. Cut tortilla in half and then cut each triangle in half. Serve immediately.

BEST-EVER PANCAKES

Pancakes are always a hit with young children. To sweeten these pancakes, this recipe uses stevia, which is a natural plant-based sweetener that doesn't cause tooth decay. To serve, spoon syrup of your choice over the top. Refrigerate any leftovers (separately) up to 1 week.

Yields 12 servings

1½ cups all-purpose unbleached flour

½ cup wheat germ

1 tablespoon baking powder

1 tablespoon powdered stevia

½ cup oat milk

¼ cup mashed sweet potatoes

¼ cup water

¼ cup extra-virgin coconut oil

1. In a medium bowl, combine flour, wheat-germ, baking powder, stevia, milk, sweet potatoes, and water. Stir until combined. If the batter is too thick, thin with a little extra water.

2. In a medium skillet over medium heat, heat oil. Scoop about ¼ cup batter for each pancake into skillet. Cook 2–4 minutes until lightly golden, then flip and cook 1–2 minutes longer until done. Transfer pancakes to a plate. Repeat with remaining batter.

3. Cut pancakes into 1" sections. Serve immediately.

HOW TO COOK A PANCAKE

Use a ¼-cup measure to scoop out the batter and pour onto a heated, greased skillet. Make sure the skillet is not too hot, or the pancakes will cook too fast and burn before the other side is cooked. Cook pancakes about 2–4 minutes until the edges start to look dry and bubbles form on the surface. Carefully flip the pancakes and cook 1–2 minutes longer until the second side is light brown.

TERIYAKI CAULIFLOWER

Because cauliflower has such a mild taste, you can flavor it with anything and it will taste great! To add protein, add a few chunks of tofu right before baking. Your child won't know the difference. This recipe pairs well with Asian Vegetable Fried Rice (see recipe in this chapter).

Yields 6 servings

1 tablespoon water
1 tablespoon cornstarch
¼ cup coconut aminos
¼ cup apple cider vinegar
1 tablespoon molasses
1 tablespoon agave nectar
1 clove garlic, peeled and minced
½ teaspoon ground ginger
12 ounces frozen cauliflower florets

1. Preheat oven to 375°F.

2. In a small bowl, combine water and cornstarch until a paste forms.

3. In a small saucepan over medium heat, combine cornstarch mixture with coconut aminos, vinegar, molasses, agave nectar, garlic, and ginger. Heat 5 minutes until bubbly, stirring frequently until thickened. Remove from heat.

4. Add cauliflower to a large casserole dish. Pour sauce over cauliflower, stirring to coat each piece. Bake 25–30 minutes until cauliflower is tender. Cool slightly.

5. Cut cauliflower into small, bite-sized pieces. Serve warm.

WHAT IS COCONUT AMINOS?

Coconut aminos is a condiment similar to soy sauce, but it's made from the fermented sap of a coconut palm tree and sea salt. The sodium content in coconut aminos is significantly lower than soy sauce. It is more expensive than soy sauce, but it's a great alternative if you're avoiding soy. It can be found in the same location as soy sauce at your local grocery store.

CABBAGE HAND PIES

These hand pies are a delicious and savory snack for your little one to enjoy. For a sweet treat, try the Cherry Hand Pies (see recipe in this chapter).

Yields 1 serving

1 cup shredded cabbage
¼ cup diced carrots
1 tablespoon vegetable stock
⅛ teaspoon salt
⅛ teaspoon ground black pepper
1 frozen puff pastry sheet, thawed
¼ cup plant-based butter, melted

1. In a medium skillet over medium-high heat, add cabbage, carrots, and stock. Season with salt and pepper. Cover and simmer 15–20 minutes until cabbage is tender. Remove from heat and set aside.

2. On a lightly floured surface, roll out the puff pastry sheet with a rolling pin to a 9" × 12" rectangle. Cut into six (3" × 4") rectangles.

3. Spoon 1 tablespoon cabbage mixture in the center of a pastry rectangle. Carefully fold pastry in half to form a half-moon shape. Press the sides together with a fork to seal. Repeat with remaining cabbage mixture and pastry.

4. Preheat oven to 350°F. Brush each pie with butter. Bake 20 minutes until golden brown. Cool 15 minutes before serving.

KALE, SWEET PEPPERS, AND RICE BOWL

Kale and sweet red bell peppers make a wonderful combination that your toddler will love.

Yields 4 servings

1 teaspoon extra-virgin olive oil
1 cup kale leaves
¼ cup diced red bell pepper
⅓ cup cooked brown rice

1. In a medium skillet over medium heat, heat oil. Add kale and pepper and sauté 5 minutes.

2. Add rice. Stir until combined.

3. Transfer the mixture to a food processor and pulse a few times to break up the kale into smaller pieces. Add water if necessary to achieve desired consistency. Alternatively, mash with a fork. Serve warm.

PEAR RISOTTO

Risotto typically takes a long time to cook, but heating up the vegetable stock before adding it to the rice speeds up the process. If you add cool vegetable stock, it may need to cook about 15 minutes longer, but the end result is worth the wait! Serve this dish with a green vegetable.

Yields 6 servings

2 tablespoons extra-virgin olive oil
1 medium Anjou pear, peeled, cored, and chopped
¼ teaspoon ground ginger
1 cup arborio rice
3 cups hot vegetable stock

1. In a large skillet over medium-high heat, heat oil. Add pear and ginger. Cook about 2 minutes, stirring until pear is soft and fragrant.

2. Add rice and cook 2 minutes until grains start to become shiny and translucent.

3. Add stock. Reduce heat to low, cover, and simmer 20 minutes until most of the liquid is absorbed. Remove from heat and cool slightly. Serve warm.

SKILLET APPLE MASH

This southern classic is known for its comforting qualities when the seasons start to change and the weather turns cold. This recipe sautés the apples in a variety of spices that will warm your heart. Serve it alone or as a topping on oatmeal or fresh biscuits.

Yields 4 servings

2 tablespoons extra-virgin coconut oil
1 cup peeled and chopped Granny Smith apple
2 tablespoons pure maple syrup
⅛ teaspoon ground cardamom
¼ teaspoon ground cinnamon
1 teaspoon vanilla extract

1. In a large skillet over medium heat, heat oil. Add remaining ingredients. Stir to combine. Cover.

2. Cook 20 minutes until apples are soft enough to mash with a fork. Remove from heat.

3. Using a fork or potato masher, mash apples until the texture is like a chunky applesauce. Serve warm.

BLACK BEAN NUGGETS

These nuggets are another great flavorful option for your little one. This recipe contains an egg, so if your plant-based diet doesn't include eggs, feel free to substitute ¼ cup ground flaxseeds or egg replacer.

Yields 4 servings

8 ounces canned black beans, drained and rinsed
¼ medium green bell pepper, seeded
¼ medium yellow onion, peeled
2 cloves garlic, peeled
½ teaspoon salt
⅛ teaspoon ground black pepper
1 large egg, lightly beaten
½ cup panko bread crumbs

1. Preheat oven to 375°F. Grease a baking sheet with nonstick cooking spray.

2. Combine beans, bell pepper, onion, garlic, salt, and black pepper in a food processor. Pulse until all ingredients are incorporated. The mixture should resemble finely chopped bits, not a purée.

3. Transfer the mixture to a medium bowl. Add egg. Stir until incorporated.

4. Using your hands, form the mixture into 1" balls and then flatten them slightly with your hands. Coat nuggets with panko crumbs and place on the prepared baking sheet.

5. Bake 5 minutes on each side. Serve warm.

BALSAMIC STRAWBERRIES WITH PLANT-POWERED YOGURT

If you have a specialty gourmet store in your area, it's worth getting the aged balsamic vinegar. It's very thick and rich and more flavorful then the watery version you find at most stores.

Yields 4 servings

¼ cup sliced strawberries
¼ teaspoon vanilla extract
1 teaspoon pure maple syrup
1 teaspoon balsamic vinegar
½ cup coconut milk yogurt alternative

1. In a medium bowl, combine strawberries, vanilla, maple syrup, and vinegar. Cover and refrigerate 30 minutes to allow the flavors to develop.

2. Fold strawberries into yogurt. Serve immediately.

BARBECUE TOFU AND QUINOA

Tofu and quinoa combine for a protein-rich meal with a smoky barbecue sauce.

Yields 6 servings

1 tablespoon extra-virgin olive oil
1 pound firm tofu, cut into 1" cubes
1 cup diced cremini mushroom caps
¼ small yellow onion, peeled and diced
1 large red bell pepper, seeded and diced
½ cup Basic Barbecue Sauce (see sidebar)
2 cups cooked quinoa

1. In a medium skillet over high heat, heat oil. Add tofu and cook 3 minutes, turning the tofu as it cooks.

2. Add mushrooms, onion, and pepper, and cook an additional 5 minutes until the vegetables are tender. Add Basic Barbecue Sauce and stir to coat. Reduce the heat and simmer 5 minutes until heated through.

3. Serve over prepared quinoa.

BASIC BARBECUE SAUCE

To make a simple yet tasty barbecue sauce, combine ¼ cup coconut aminos, 2 tablespoons blackstrap molasses, 3 tablespoons pure maple syrup, 2 teaspoons hickory liquid smoke, ½ teaspoon garlic powder, ½ teaspoon onion powder, ¼ teaspoon ground black pepper, and ¼ cup ketchup. Simmer over low heat 20 minutes and enjoy!

CRISPY TOFU NUGGETS

No one will know that these crispy nuggets are not meat! Tofu nuggets are high in protein, and kids love them. You can also make these in an air fryer if you have one! Serve with a variety of your favorite prepared plant-based dipping sauces, including organic ketchup, barbecue sauce, or honey-mustard sauce.

Yields 4 servings

½ cup oat milk
3 cups crushed store-bought crispy onion strings
½ cup chickpea flour
1 (14-ounce) block firm or extra-firm tofu
Extra-virgin olive oil cooking spray

1. Preheat your oven to 400°F. Line a baking sheet with foil and set aside.

2. Place milk in a shallow bowl. In a separate shallow bowl, combine onion strings and chickpea flour. Set aside.

3. Drain the tofu and pat dry with paper towels. Cut tofu into ½" slices and press flat into nuggets with your hands. Place nuggets in a single layer onto wax paper and freeze 20 minutes.

4. Submerge one nugget in milk, then dredge it in the onion strings, using a spoon to coat all sides. Place nugget on prepared baking sheet. Repeat until all nuggets are coated.

5. Spray nuggets with olive oil spray. Bake 3-4 minutes on each side until golden brown. Remove from heat. Serve warm.

BANANA COCONUT DE LECHE

When you want to give your toddler a refreshing yet healthy beverage, try this recipe. He'll get the health benefits from the fresh banana and nutritious coconut milk, making it the perfect choice over any sugary drink.

Yields 1 serving

¼ cup unsweetened carton coconut milk
½ medium banana, peeled and broken into large pieces
¼ teaspoon ground cinnamon

Combine all ingredients in a blender. Blend 30 seconds. Serve immediately.

AVOCADO ZOODLES

You can purchase spiralized zucchini from the freshly prepared cut vegetable section of the grocery, or spiralize the zucchini yourself using a spiralizer tool.

Yields 2 servings

¼ cup mashed avocado

¼ teaspoon fresh lime juice

2 teaspoons plant-based butter

1 cup spiralized zucchini

2 tablespoons diced tomatoes

1 teaspoon diced red onion

1 clove garlic, peeled and minced

3 tablespoons unsweetened carton coconut milk

1. In a small bowl, combine mashed avocado and lime juice. Set aside.

2. In a small saucepan over medium-low heat, warm butter. Add zucchini and cook 5 minutes until heated through.

3. Add avocado and remaining ingredients. Cook about 5 minutes until heated through. Before serving, cut the zoodles into smaller, chewable pieces. Serve warm.

SWAP IT

You can use whole-wheat pasta or any other type of plant-based pasta such as chickpea, black bean, or edamame noodles in place of the zucchini noodles. Because bean-flour-based pastas offer a lot of protein and other nutritious benefits, it's a healthy swap. Stay away from refined pasta, though.

GARLIC NAAN VEGETABLE PIZZA SQUARES
(PICTURED)

This recipe uses naan bread as a pizza crust with a garlicky basil spread. Many stores carry naan along with other specialty breads. Feel free to use whatever crust you like! Prepared options include cauliflower, traditional wheat flour, and pita bread, all of which can be used as pizza crust.

Yields 4 servings

1 tablespoon extra-virgin olive oil
4 cloves garlic, peeled and minced
1 teaspoon dried basil
⅛ teaspoon salt
1 slice naan bread
¼ cup diced baby bella mushrooms
1 tablespoon diced red onion
1 tablespoon diced red bell pepper
1 tablespoon diced green bell pepper
1 tablespoon diced black olives

1. Preheat oven to 375°F.

2. In a small bowl, combine oil, garlic, basil, and salt. Let stand 10 minutes to allow the flavors to develop.

3. Using a pastry brush or the back of a spoon, spread oil mixture on one side of naan bread until completely covered.

4. Sprinkle remaining vegetables on top of bread. Transfer pizza to a baking sheet and bake 8 minutes.

5. Cut pizza into squares. Serve immediately.

CUCUMBER BITES

If your toddler isn't sold on cucumbers, try adding a little dill to the slices. This snack is a favorite among even the pickiest little eaters.

Yields 4 servings

½ medium English cucumber, halved
¼ teaspoon dill weed

1. Cut the cucumber lengthwise into small sticks about half the size of your pinky finger.

2. Sprinkle sparingly with dill. Serve as a finger food.

GARLIC AND BASIL GRITS

Although not your traditional breakfast grits, these savory grits are just as delicious for dinner and introduce some new flavors for your child to enjoy.

Yields 2 servings

¼ cup uncooked grits

1 cup Vegetable Stock, plus more for thinning (see recipe in Chapter 4)

1 teaspoon pressed garlic

1 teaspoon dried basil

2 teaspoons plant-based butter

⅛ teaspoon salt

1. In a medium saucepan over medium heat, combine all ingredients. Bring to a boil, stirring constantly.

2. Reduce heat to low, cover, and simmer 5–6 minutes until liquid is absorbed. Add additional stock to thin, if needed.

3. Serve warm.

ORZO AND COLLARD GREEN MASH

This hearty and savory dish is easy to pull together any night of the week. It is the perfect blend of leafy greens, pasta, and Italian flavors.

Yields 4 servings

4 cups trimmed collard greens

2 cups vegetable stock

2 tablespoons chopped yellow onion

3 cloves garlic, peeled and pressed

1 tablespoon extra-virgin olive oil

1 cup cooked orzo

½ teaspoon Italian seasoning

1. In a medium saucepan over medium-high heat, add collards, stock, onion, garlic, and oil.

2. Boil about 25 minutes until collards are extremely tender. Remove from heat.

3. Mash collards with a fork, or use a knife to cut into small pieces. Toss with orzo and Italian seasoning. Serve warm.

CABBAGE AND RICE SKILLET

This skillet is a great way to use up any leftover brown rice. When time is short, you can whip up this delicious meal in less than 15 minutes!

Yields 1 serving

2 tablespoons vegetable stock
2 teaspoons plant-based butter
½ cup finely chopped cabbage
2 tablespoons grated carrot
1 tablespoon diced yellow onion
¼ cup cooked brown rice
⅛ teaspoon salt
⅛ teaspoon ground black pepper

1. In a large skillet over medium heat, heat stock and butter. Add cabbage, carrot, and onion. Cover and cook 10 minutes until cabbage is tender.

2. Add rice and stir to combine. Cook an additional 3 minutes until heated through. Sprinkle with salt and pepper. Serve warm.

BUTTERNUT SQUASH AND KALE CHIP CRUNCH

This recipe adds the crunch that toddlers love. Squash and kale unite in this delicious finger-food snack.

Yields 3 servings

½ cup cubed butternut squash
1 bunch kale, torn into 1" pieces, stems removed
½ tablespoon extra-virgin olive oil
1 teaspoon salt
½ teaspoon garlic powder

1. Preheat oven to 375°F.

2. Arrange squash in a small baking dish and bake 20 minutes until fork-tender.

3. Arrange kale in a single layer on a baking sheet. Drizzle with oil and sprinkle with salt and garlic powder.

4. Bake about 10 minutes until the outer edges of leaves turn brown. The leaves will crisp more as they stand.

5. Toss the squash cubes and kale together. Serve immediately.

GRILLED PINEAPPLE TOPPED WITH COCONUT-BANANA FREEZE

This healthy dessert is packed with nutritional benefits—potassium, fat, and vitamin C, just to name a few. Best of all, there is no added sugar! You'll need frozen bananas on hand. To freeze, simply peel the bananas and freeze them whole in a freezer-safe container at least 12 hours. You can freeze bananas up to 8 weeks!

Yields 6 servings

1 (13.5-ounce) can unsweetened coconut milk

2 large frozen bananas, broken in half

1 (15-ounce) can pineapple slices in juice, juice reserved

½ teaspoon ground cinnamon, divided

1. Open the can of coconut milk (do not shake it first!). Skim the cream from the top and place in a food processor. Save the remaining coconut water for another use.

2. Add bananas, pineapple juice from can, and ¼ teaspoon cinnamon to the food processor. Process until smooth and creamy (similar to soft-serve ice cream). Transfer to a freezer-safe container. Freeze 3 hours.

3. In a medium skillet over medium-high heat, place six pineapple slices. Sprinkle with remaining ¼ teaspoon cinnamon. Cook 1 minute on each side.

4. Place one pineapple slice in a bowl and top with ¼ cup banana freeze. Serve immediately.

RECIPE NOTE

This recipe makes enough for everyone. The banana freeze is good enough to eat on its own or combined with other purées in this book as a healthy dessert option.

PINEAPPLE STEEL-CUT OATS

Steel-cut oats are quite different from old-fashioned oats, and it's good to give both varieties a try. Steel-cut oats are less processed than traditional oats and they have a chewier bite. They are just as delicious when mixed with pineapple for a tropical flare.

Yields 1 serving

2 tablespoons crushed canned pineapple

¼ cup steel-cut oats

¼ cup unsweetened carton coconut milk, plus more for thinning

½ cup water

1. In a small saucepan over medium heat, combine all ingredients. Bring to a boil.

2. Reduce the heat to low, cover and simmer 10–15 minutes until water is absorbed. Add additional milk to thin if needed. Serve warm.

CURRIED VEGETABLES

Add a little green to this recipe with a sprig of parsley or broccoli florets for a beautiful presentation.

Yields 3 servings

2 tablespoons mild red curry paste

1 teaspoon extra-virgin olive oil

1 cup cauliflower florets

½ cup chopped carrots

½ cup unsweetened canned coconut milk

1 large white potato, peeled and diced

1 cup vegetable stock

1. In a medium saucepan over medium heat, combine curry paste and oil. Cook 2–3 minutes, watching carefully to make sure it doesn't burn.

2. Add remaining ingredients and stir to combine. Simmer 25–30 minutes until all the vegetables are fork-tender. Stir occasionally to prevent sticking.

3. Allow to cool, then fork-mash before serving.

CREAMY DREAMY TORTELLINI

Choose any type of prepared tortellini for this recipe. Tortellini is typically made with eggs and filled with some type of cheese, but if your plant-based lifestyle doesn't include any animal products, there are vegan alternatives that you can find at the health food store.

Yields 8 servings

12 ounces uncooked refrigerated tortellini
1 tablespoon extra-virgin olive oil
1 small yellow onion, peeled and chopped
½ cup chopped baby bella mushrooms
1 clove garlic, peeled and minced
1 (15-ounce) can diced tomatoes
1 teaspoon salt
¼ teaspoon ground black pepper
1½ teaspoons dried basil
2 cups unsweetened carton coconut milk
2 tablespoons organic all-purpose unbleached flour
1 cup packed baby spinach
1 sprig fresh parsley

1. Cook tortellini according to package directions. Drain and set aside.

2. In a medium skillet over medium heat, heat oil. Add onion and mushrooms and sauté until tender, about 2 minutes. Add garlic, tomatoes, salt, pepper, and basil. Simmer 10 minutes.

3. In a medium bowl, whisk together milk and flour. Add to skillet with tomato mixture along with spinach. Stir to combine. Cook 3 minutes until heated through.

4. Add tortellini. Stir to coat. Reduce heat to low and simmer about 5 minutes until thickened. Garnish with parsley. Serve immediately.

PARSNIP STICKS

These parsnip sticks are sautéed soft for your toddler to pick up and self-feed. Remember to purchase smaller yet firm parsnips to prepare, as they tend to be less bitter than the larger sizes. Parsnips should be thinly sliced to speed up the cooking process.

Yields 6 servings

2 teaspoons extra-virgin olive oil (or olive oil cooking spray), plus more for sautéing if needed

½ teaspoon minced garlic

½ tablespoon finely chopped chives

4 medium parsnips, peeled and cut into ¼" matchsticks

⅛ teaspoon salt

⅛ teaspoon ground black pepper

1. In a small mixing bowl, combine 2 teaspoons oil, garlic, and chives. Stir to combine. Add parsnips and, using your hands, thoroughly coat them with the oil mixture.

2. To a large skillet over medium heat, add coated parsnips. Sauté, stirring occasionally, about 10 minutes until parsnips are tender and browning around the ends. Add more oil if the skillet becomes dry. Alternatively, you can spray them with olive oil cooking spray. Season with salt and pepper. Serve immediately.

UNICORN NICE CREAM
(PICTURED)

This magical frozen treat is sure to please! It gets its blue color from the nutritious spirulina. Your little one will look forward to this healthy, plant-based soft-serve.

Yields 4 servings

2 medium frozen bananas, chopped

½ cup frozen chopped mango

1 tablespoon blue spirulina powder

½ cup cold unsweetened canned coconut milk, plus more for thinning

1 tablespoon cold canned coconut cream

1. Combine all ingredients in a food processor. Blend until completely smooth, pushing the chunks toward the blades to process if necessary. Add more milk if needed to churn the soft-serve until it looks like a whirlpool. Serve immediately.

2. Transfer remaining nice cream to a freezer-safe container and freeze.

SWEET POTATO BALLS

These sweet potato balls really deliver on taste and resemble little snowballs when coated with the coconut. They are a healthy treat full of beta-carotene, fiber, and healthy antioxidants. Pile them up on a plate and enjoy!

Yields 6 servings

2 medium sweet potatoes, peeled and cut into ½" cubes

2 tablespoons water

2 tablespoons unsweetened canned coconut milk

½ teaspoon minced garlic

¼ teaspoon ground cinnamon

2 tablespoons ground flaxseeds

¼ cup unsweetened coconut flakes

1. Preheat oven to 400°F. Spray a baking sheet with nonstick cooking spray.

2. In a medium nonstick saucepan over medium-low heat, add sweet potatoes and water. Cover and simmer 15 minutes, stirring occasionally until potatoes are easily pierced with a fork. Remove from heat.

3. Add milk and mash potatoes with a fork. Add garlic, cinnamon, and flaxseeds. Mix well. Form potato mixture into 1½" balls.

4. Place coconut flakes in a small bowl and dredge balls in coconut. Arrange balls on prepared baking sheet in a single layer.

5. Bake 15 minutes until coconut is toasted. Serve immediately.

EASY PLANT-BASED SPAGHETTI

Pick your favorite organic spaghetti sauce from the grocery store for an easy plant-based spaghetti dish that no one would ever know was made from chickpeas. Chickpea pasta takes center stage with the healthy nutrition it provides, and it's gluten-free too!

Yields 3 servings

¼ cup cooked chickpea spaghetti pasta, cut into 1" pieces

⅓ cup store-bought organic spaghetti sauce

1 clove garlic, peeled and minced

1 teaspoon chopped fresh parsley

In a small saucepan over medium heat, combine all ingredients. Cover and cook until heated through, about 5 minutes. Stir occasionally. Serve warm.

CHICKPEA GYRO

Your little one will have fun deconstructing this gyro. Serve it like a pita and watch the magic of self-feeding and exploration.

Yields 2 servings

⅓ cup canned chickpeas, drained and rinsed
¼ teaspoon chopped fresh rosemary
¼ teaspoon dried oregano
¼ teaspoon sweet paprika
2 teaspoons extra-virgin olive oil
½ pita bread
1 tablespoon garlic hummus
¼ cup diced Roma tomato
¼ cup diced cucumber

1. In a small bowl, combine chickpeas, rosemary, oregano, and paprika.

2. In a medium skillet over medium heat, heat oil. Add chickpea mixture and cook about 8 minutes, stirring occasionally, until chickpeas are golden brown. Remove from heat.

3. Spread garlic hummus on top of pita bread. Add tomato and cucumber, then chickpeas. Cut pita in half and serve.

APPLE-CHIA CUSTARD

There is such a thing as having a custard without the dairy, and this recipe is proof! Coconut milk is a wonderful replacement for cow's milk. The full-fat version that comes in a can provides enough fat to make it suitable for baking and whipping up delicious, rich custard.

Yields 2 servings

½ cup Apple Purée (see recipe in Chapter 4)
¼ teaspoon chia seeds
¼ teaspoon ground cardamom
½ cup unsweetened canned coconut milk
2 teaspoons vanilla extract
2 teaspoons honey
1 teaspoon tapioca flour

1. In a small bowl, combine Apple Purée, chia seeds, and cardamom. Set aside.

2. In a small saucepan over medium heat, combine milk, vanilla, and honey. Bring to a boil, stirring frequently. Simmer 3 minutes.

3. Vigorously whisk in flour until the mixture thickens. If the mixture isn't thick enough, add another teaspoon flour; if it's too thick, add another teaspoon milk. The mixture should resemble a soft pudding. Remove from heat and allow to cool 5–10 minutes.

4. Fold in apple mixture to combine. Serve warm or chilled.

CHICKPEA ROTINI PASTA WITH MUSHROOM SAUCE

The best thing about oat milk is that it doesn't add a flavor to meals. It's the best choice in place of cow's milk if you don't want to alter the taste of recipes. Purchase the extra-creamy oat milk for a beautifully textured sauce.

Yields 3 servings

1 teaspoon plant-based butter

¼ cup chopped baby bella mushrooms

1 teaspoon minced garlic

2 tablespoons oat milk

¼ cup cooked chickpea rotini pasta

1. In a small saucepan over medium heat, warm butter. Add mushrooms and garlic and sauté 5 minutes until mushrooms are cooked through.

2. Add milk and stir to combine. Reduce heat to low and simmer 10 minutes to allow flavors to combine. Stir in pasta. Cook an additional 5 minutes. Serve warm.

SIMPLE TOFU WITH APRICOT

This high-protein purée takes on the flavor of apricot and doesn't disappoint. Serve it for breakfast or as a spread for Homemade Biter Biscuits (see recipe in this chapter).

Yields 15 servings

½ cup silken tofu

2 tablespoons Apricot Purée (see recipe in Chapter 4)

⅛ teaspoon ground cinnamon

Add all ingredients to a food processor. Blend to a chunky consistency. Serve immediately.

THREE-BEAN SALAD

It's important to prepare this salad the day before you want to serve it because it has to marinate in the refrigerator for the beans to absorb the dressing and become flavorful. It's definitely worth the wait!

Yields 8 servings

¼ cup extra-virgin olive oil

⅓ cup apple cider vinegar

½ teaspoon dry mustard

½ teaspoon salt

⅛ teaspoon ground black pepper

¼ cup minced red onion

1 clove garlic, peeled and minced

1 tablespoon honey

1 (15-ounce) can green beans, drained and rinsed

1 (15-ounce) can black beans, drained and rinsed

1 (15-ounce) can chickpeas, drained and rinsed

1. In a salad bowl, whisk together oil, vinegar, mustard, salt, pepper, onion, garlic, and honey.

2. Add all beans to salad bowl and toss gently to coat. Cover and refrigerate overnight before serving. Refrigerate leftovers up to 3 days.

MELON PICK-ME-UPS

For this recipe, the melon pieces should be small, bite-sized cubes that your toddlers can pick up with their hands and feed themselves. You can serve this dish either alone or with small bites of avocado.

Yields 2 servings

½ cup cubed honeydew melon

½ cup cubed cantaloupe

Toss all ingredients in a small bowl. Serve immediately.

LOADED AVOCADO WITH FRUIT

This chunky purée is a take on loaded potatoes, but this one is made with avocado and fruit. Avocado pairs well with many different fruit flavors; here we've combined it into something your toddler will look forward to.

Yields 2 servings

5 slices banana
2 large strawberries, hulled and sliced
¼ cup mashed avocado
1 tablespoon diced cucumber
2 mint leaves, finely chopped
2 teaspoons unsweetened grated coconut

1. In a small bowl, combine banana and strawberries. Fork-mash into a chunky texture.

2. In your serving dish, add avocado and layer bananas and strawberries, cucumber, and mint. Sprinkle coconut on top. Serve immediately.

MINI STUFFED SWEET PEPPERS

Ditch the dairy cream cheese for a healthier, plant-based cream cheese made with cashews and coconut. A great brand to try is Miyoko's. Make sure your family has no allergies to cashews or coconut before serving this delicious snack.

Yields 9 servings

3 miniature red, orange, or yellow bell peppers, stemmed, seeded, and sliced in half
2 ounces vegan garlic-chive cream cheese spread

Fill each pepper half with the cream cheese spread. Serve immediately.

SUNFLOWER SEED BUTTER AND YOGURT

Sunflower seed butter is a great alternative to peanut butter. It has a similar consistency and nutty flavor. When combined with oat milk yogurt or any other yogurt alternative, it's a healthy snack with lots of fat and nutrition.

Yields 1 serving

1 tablespoon sunflower seed butter

¼ cup oat milk yogurt alternative

¼ teaspoon ground cinnamon

In a small bowl, combine all ingredients. Serve immediately.

ASIAN VEGETABLE FRIED RICE

Serve Asian fare at home with this yummy fried rice recipe. Sesame oil brings many health benefits. It aids in bone growth and has anti-inflammatory properties.

Yields 3 servings

1 tablespoon sesame oil

2 tablespoons grated carrots

¼ cup cooked brown rice, cold

2 tablespoons fresh or thawed frozen sweet peas

1 teaspoon minced garlic

⅛ teaspoon ground ginger

1 tablespoon vegetable stock

1. In a medium skillet over medium heat, heat oil. Add remaining ingredients and sauté about 5 minutes. Remove from heat.

2. Fork-mash or add to blender and pulse for a chunky purée. Add more stock to thin as needed. Serve warm.

CHERRY HAND PIES
(PICTURED)

These hand pies are a favorite among young eaters! The light and airy puff pastry is especially tasty, and when combined with the cherry preserves it's a match made in heaven! You can find puff pastry sheets in the freezer section near prepared piecrusts.

Yields 9 servings

1 frozen puff pastry sheet, thawed
1 (13-ounce) jar cherry preserves
¼ cup plant-based butter, melted

1. Preheat oven to 350°F.

2. On a lightly floured surface, roll out puff pastry sheet into a 9" × 12" rectangle. Cut nine (3" × 4") rectangles.

3. Spoon 1 tablespoon cherry preserves in the center of one pastry rectangle. Carefully fold one side of the pastry to the other, forming a half-moon shape. Press the sides together with a fork to seal. Repeat with remaining pastry rectangles.

4. Brush each pastry with melted butter. Bake 20 minutes until golden brown. Cool 15 minutes before serving.

BREADED CAULIFLOWER

Kids love crunchy foods, and this breaded cauliflower will win over your little one. Who needs processed chicken nuggets when you can make this healthy vegetable that packs a lot of crunch? Serve alone or with your favorite dressing or dip. You can use broccoli instead of cauliflower!

Yields 4 servings

1 cup oat milk
¼ cup panko bread crumbs
1 teaspoon dried parsley
1 teaspoon garlic powder
1 cup cauliflower florets, cut in half lengthwise

1. Preheat oven to 400°F.

2. In a shallow dish, add milk. In a separate shallow dish, combine panko crumbs, parsley, and garlic powder.

3. Dunk a cauliflower floret in milk, then dredge in panko mixture. Repeat with remaining florets.

4. Arrange cauliflower in a single layer on a nonstick baking sheet. Bake 20 minutes. Cool 5 minutes. Serve warm as a finger food.

PEACH AND COCONUT SORBET

It's hard to find plant-based ice cream that doesn't have a ton of sugar. This recipe takes advantage of the natural sweetness in peaches and banana to make a healthy frozen treat that you can feel good about serving!

Yields 10 servings

1 (13.5-ounce) can unsweetened coconut milk
1 (12-ounce) bag frozen peaches
1 medium frozen banana

1. Open the can of coconut milk (do not shake it first!). Skim the cream from the top and place in a food processor. Reserve remaining coconut water for another use.

2. Add peaches and banana. Process about 5 minutes until smooth.

3. Using a spoon, check for any large pieces. Continue processing if large pieces remain. When there are no large pieces left, transfer mixture to a freezer-safe container.

4. Chill 1 hour before serving.

BREAD PUDDING BONANZA

Use leftover bread for this recipe, even if it's gone stale. The baking process softens it up and offers a nice texture that's easy for baby to eat. Serve your portion with caramel or chocolate sauce on top!

Yields 2 servings

4 slices leftover bread, diced
¼ cup mashed banana
½ cup oat milk
1 tablespoon plant-based butter, melted
3 tablespoons pure maple syrup
½ teaspoon vanilla extract
¼ teaspoon ground cinnamon

1. Preheat oven to 350°F. Grease a medium baking dish.

2. Place bread cubes in prepared baking dish.

3. In a medium bowl, combine banana, milk, butter, maple syrup, vanilla, and cinnamon. Pour over bread cubes and let soak 10 minutes.

4. Bake 45 minutes until a toothpick inserted into the center comes out clean. Allow to cool and serve warm.

SOULFUL GRITS

Note that if you want to feed grits to your baby when she's younger than 10 months, you'll need to stick to the instant variety. Traditional grits will be too gritty.

Yields 2 servings

¼ cup uncooked grits

1 cup Vegetable Stock (see recipe in Chapter 4)

1 tablespoon nutritional yeast

1 tablespoon plant-based butter

⅛ teaspoon salt

⅛ teaspoon ground black pepper

1. In a small saucepan over medium-high heat, combine grits and Vegetable Stock. Bring to a boil, stirring constantly. Add yeast, butter, salt, and pepper.

2. Reduce heat, cover, and simmer 5 minutes.

3. Serve warm.

ZUCCHINI, CARROT, AND COUSCOUS MEDLEY

This dish is packed with protein and healthy fat. You know you're giving your baby the best when you prepare this nutritious—and delicious—dish.

Yields 8 servings

1 cup whole-wheat couscous

1 cup water

2 tablespoons plus 1 teaspoon extra-virgin olive oil, divided

1 teaspoon ground flaxseeds

½ teaspoon minced garlic

1 cup canned white beans

½ cup grated zucchini

½ cup carrot rounds

1. In a medium microwave-safe bowl, combine couscous, water, and 2 tablespoons oil. Cover and microwave on high 2–3 minutes. Fluff with fork. Sprinkle flaxseeds on couscous and blend with fork. Set aside.

2. In a medium saucepan over medium heat, heat remaining 1 teaspoon oil. Add garlic and sauté until translucent.

3. Add beans, zucchini, and carrots, and sauté 5 minutes. Mash with fork or purée to a chunky consistency.

4. Combine vegetable mixture with couscous and serve.

BAKED PITA CHIPS

These make great chips for snacking. Serve these with Chocolate-Pomegranate Dip (see recipe in this chapter).

Yields 48 chips (8 servings)

6 whole-wheat pita pockets
½ cup extra-virgin olive oil
½ teaspoon garlic salt

1. Preheat oven to 400°F.

2. Lay out pitas and brush both sides with oil. Cut each pita into eight chips.

3. Sprinkle with garlic salt. Spread pita chips out on a baking sheet.

4. Bake about 7 minutes until pitas turn brown and crispy. Cool on a wire rack. Serve immediately.

CHOCOLATE-POMEGRANATE DIP

Commercial pomegranate juice is filled with antioxidants. It's also an amazing source of potassium, which helps your kidneys, heart, and muscles work correctly.

Yields 3 cups (12 servings)

1 (3.7-ounce) package organic instant chocolate pudding
1½ cups unsweetened canned coconut milk
⅓ cup 100 percent pomegranate juice
½ teaspoon orange zest

1. In a medium mixing bowl, using a whisk or electric mixer on low speed combine chocolate pudding mix and milk.

2. Add remaining ingredients and blend until smooth, about 2 minutes.

3. Pour into small serving bowls or one large bowl. Refrigerate 1 hour until set and serve.

BAKED TORTILLA CHIPS

Making your own tortilla chips is rewarding, especially if you can't find already made organic chips at the store. Serve these chips with Pineapple Salsa (see recipe in this chapter). Use whole-wheat tortillas instead of corn, or make them both and mix them up!

Yields 40 chips (5 servings)

Canola oil, for drizzling
5 (6") corn tortillas
Sprinkle sea salt

1. Preheat oven to 350°F. Drizzle a large baking sheet with oil.

2. Cut tortillas into eight wedges each. Spread tortilla wedges on prepared baking sheet in a single layer.

3. Drizzle tops of tortilla wedges with oil and sprinkle with sea salt.

4. Bake 13–15 minutes until golden and crispy. Cool on a wire rack. Serve immediately.

GRILLED SUMMER VEGETABLES

Grill vegetables on the top rack of the grill if you have one for best results. Otherwise, place them in aluminum foil or in a grill pan so they won't burn or fall through the grate.

Yields 4 servings

1 medium head broccoli, trimmed into florets
1 medium yellow summer squash, trimmed and sliced
3 medium tomatoes, cored and cut into wedges
1 medium red onion, peeled and sliced
Extra-virgin olive oil, for rub
¼ teaspoon sea salt

1. Preheat grill.

2. Combine all ingredients in a large bowl, taking care to rub oil into vegetables. Wrap vegetables in aluminum foil.

3. Place on top rack of hot grill and cook 5–7 minutes until vegetables are tender. Serve immediately.

TOFU WITH ORZO IN TOMATO-SPINACH SAUCE

If you've been cooking with tofu, you know how easy it is to incorporate into so many different meals without adding unwanted flavors. It blends right in and is barely noticeable.

Yields 6 servings

¾ cup uncooked orzo pasta
½ cup Marinara Sauce (see recipe in Chapter 6)
½ cup diced silken tofu
½ cup chopped baby spinach

1. Cook orzo according to the package directions. Drain and set aside.

2. In a small saucepan over medium heat, combine Marinara Sauce, tofu, and spinach. Cook 5 minutes until heated through.

3. To serve, place a portion of orzo in a bowl and top with sauce. Serve warm.

NUTS BE GONE TRAIL MIX

This nutless trail mix is great to keep on hand to grab and go—or for serving nut-sensitive toddlers or their friends. Pack in advance using reusable snack cups, and your toddler can enjoy this yummy, energizing snack all week.

Yields 10 servings

1 cup puffed rice cereal
1 cup pretzels
½ cup dried cranberries
¼ cup sunflower seeds
2 tablespoons dark chocolate chips

In a large bowl, combine all ingredients. Serve immediately. Store leftovers in an airtight container up to 6 months.

ROASTED POTATO ROUNDS

A quick way to coat the potatoes with oil is to combine them and the olive oil in a plastic bag and shake them all up! Give the dish a splash of color by adding fresh parsley from your garden.

Yields 24 rounds (6 servings)

2 tablespoons extra-virgin olive oil, divided
3 large red-skinned potatoes, thinly sliced
Sprinkle salt
Sprinkle ground black pepper

1. Preheat oven to 475°F. Spread 1 tablespoon oil on baking sheet.

2. Spread potato slices on prepared baking sheet.

3. Drizzle with remaining 1 tablespoon oil and sprinkle with salt and pepper.

4. Bake 13–15 minutes until tender and golden. Serve warm.

PINEAPPLE SALSA

Instead of adding plain pineapple to this salsa, how about grilling it first? Cut fresh pineapple into ½"-thick slices. Place on medium-hot grill and grill 5–7 minutes per side. Cool about 10 minutes before adding to dish.

Yields 12 servings

1 cup diced fresh pineapple
½ cup diced red bell pepper
½ cup diced yellow bell pepper
½ cup black beans, drained and rinsed
¼ cup diced red onion
¼ cup finely chopped fresh cilantro
¼ cup orange-pineapple juice
2 tablespoons fresh lime juice
⅛ teaspoon salt
⅛ teaspoon ground black pepper

1. In a large bowl, combine pineapple, bell peppers, beans, onion, and cilantro. Mix well.

2. In a small bowl, combine orange-pineapple juice and lime juice. Add to large bowl.

3. Mix all ingredients together, and season with salt and pepper. Serve immediately.

BABY BISCOTTI

While you may like biscotti dipped in chocolate or nuts to go with your coffee, your baby will appreciate this hard yet comforting delight to smash against her gums.

Yields 8 servings

1 cup all-purpose unbleached flour
2 tablespoons pure maple syrup
½ teaspoon baking powder
¼ teaspoon baking soda
1 egg yolk replacer
1 tablespoon coconut oil
⅓ cup oat milk

1. Preheat oven to 325°F. Grease a baking sheet.

2. In a large bowl, mix together flour, maple syrup, baking powder, and baking soda.

3. Add egg yolk replacer, oil, and milk. Stir until the mixture forms a firm dough.

4. Shape dough into a log about 6" long. Place on prepared baking sheet, and press the log into a bar about 2" wide. Bake 20 minutes; then let stand until bar is cool enough to touch.

5. Cut diagonally into ½" slices. Spread slices out on baking sheet and bake another 10–15 minutes until slices are crispy and dry.

6. Cool on a wire rack. Serve immediately.

EGG SUBSTITUTES

Bob's Red Mill Egg Replacer can be substituted for eggs in any recipe. Look for it in your local grocery store or online. It's a gluten-free powder made from potato starch, tapioca flour, baking soda, and psyllium husk fiber. You can also use ¼ cup mashed sweet potato, pumpkin, banana, or avocado to replace eggs in recipes.

HOMEMADE BITER BISCUITS

Why settle for store-bought teething biscuits when you can make your own plant-based version? Keep these on hand when your baby wants something to chew on. The end result should be hard and crunchy. If it crumbles and breaks, it's too soft for baby.

Yields 20 servings

⅔ cup oat milk
¼ cup plant-based butter, melted and cooled
1 tablespoon pure maple syrup
1 cup wheat germ
1 cup whole-wheat flour

1. Preheat oven to 350°F. Grease a baking sheet.

2. In a medium bowl, beat together milk, butter, and maple syrup.

3. Stir in wheat germ and flour, and knead 8-10 minutes until dough is smooth and satiny. Add more milk or more flour if necessary.

4. Make small balls of dough and roll them into sticks that are about ½" thick and 4" long.

5. Bake 45 minutes until biscuits are hard and browned. Cool on a wire rack. Serve immediately.

BISCUIT SAFETY

Wait until your baby comfortably eats solid puréed foods before offering her biscuits and rusks. Always supervise your baby carefully while she's eating one—ideally she'll gnaw on the hard biscuit, getting relief for her sore gums while eating some of it, very slowly, in the process. It's always possible that she could break off a piece big enough to choke on, so be careful.

TEETHING BISCUITS

Teething biscuits, also called rusks, are a type of hard biscuit perfect for teething because they absorb the saliva from baby's mouth. That means less of it getting on you!

Yields 8 servings

¼ cup plant-based butter, softened
1 cup self-rising flour
¼ cup mashed sweet potato
¼ cup oat milk

1. Preheat oven to 375°F. Lightly grease a baking sheet.

2. In a medium bowl, using a fork, combine butter and flour. Mix together until coarse crumbs are formed.

3. Add sweet potato and milk. Stir until it forms a smooth dough, adding more or less milk as necessary.

4. Roll dough to a 1"-thick rectangle on a lightly floured surface. Cut into 1" slices and place on prepared baking sheet.

5. Bake 20–25 minutes until browned. Cool on a wire rack. Serve immediately.

SWAP IT

If your diet allows eggs, feel free to swap the mashed sweet potato in this recipe for 1 egg yolk or egg yolk replacer. The end result will be richer and a different texture with a boost of protein.

12+ MONTHS

STANDARD US/METRIC
MEASUREMENT CONVERSIONS

VOLUME CONVERSIONS

US Volume Measure	Metric Equivalent
⅛ teaspoon	0.5 milliliter
¼ teaspoon	1 milliliter
½ teaspoon	2 milliliters
1 teaspoon	5 milliliters
½ tablespoon	7 milliliters
1 tablespoon (3 teaspoons)	15 milliliters
2 tablespoons (1 fluid ounce)	30 milliliters
¼ cup (4 tablespoons)	60 milliliters
⅓ cup	90 milliliters
½ cup (4 fluid ounces)	125 milliliters
⅔ cup	160 milliliters
¾ cup (6 fluid ounces)	180 milliliters
1 cup (16 tablespoons)	250 milliliters
1 pint (2 cups)	500 milliliters
1 quart (4 cups)	1 liter (about)

WEIGHT CONVERSIONS

US Weight Measure	Metric Equivalent
½ ounce	15 grams
1 ounce	30 grams
2 ounces	60 grams
3 ounces	85 grams
¼ pound (4 ounces)	115 grams
½ pound (8 ounces)	225 grams
¾ pound (12 ounces)	340 grams
1 pound (16 ounces)	454 grams

OVEN TEMPERATURE CONVERSIONS

Degrees Fahrenheit	Degrees Celsius
200 degrees F	95 degrees C
250 degrees F	120 degrees C
275 degrees F	135 degrees C
300 degrees F	150 degrees C
325 degrees F	160 degrees C
350 degrees F	180 degrees C
375 degrees F	190 degrees C
400 degrees F	205 degrees C
425 degrees F	220 degrees C
450 degrees F	230 degrees C

BAKING PAN SIZES

American	Metric
8 × 1½ inch round baking pan	20 × 4 cm cake tin
9 × 1½ inch round baking pan	23 × 3.5 cm cake tin
11 × 7 × 1½ inch baking pan	28 × 18 × 4 cm baking tin
13 × 9 × 2 inch baking pan	30 × 20 × 5 cm baking tin
2 quart rectangular baking dish	30 × 20 × 3 cm baking tin
15 × 10 × 2 inch baking pan	30 × 25 × 2 cm baking tin (Swiss roll tin)
9 inch pie plate	22 × 4 or 23 × 4 cm pie plate
7 or 8 inch springform pan	18 or 20 cm springform or loose bottom cake tin
9 × 5 × 3 inch loaf pan	23 × 13 × 7 cm or 2 lb narrow loaf or pâté tin
1½ quart casserole	1.5 liter casserole
2 quart casserole	2 liter casserole

INDEX

Note: Page numbers in **bold** indicate recipe category lists.